FIELD GUIDE TO THE

INTERNET

PUBLISHED BY

Microsoft Press
A Division of Microsoft Corporation
One Microsoft Way
Redmond, Washington 98052-6399

Library of Congress Cataloging-in-Publication Data
Nelson, Stephen L., 1959-
  Field guide to Microsoft Field Guide to the Internet /
  Stephen L. Nelson.
      p.   cm.
  Includes index.
  ISBN 1-55615-822-X
  1. Internet (Computer Network)   I. Title.
TK5105.875.I57N45 1995
004.6'7--dc20   95-31107
                                          CIP

Printed and bound in the United States of America.

1 2 3 4 5 6 7 8 9 OBP 9 8 7 5 6 4

Distributed to the book trade in Canada by Macmillan of
Canada, a division of Canada Publishing Corporation.

A CIP catalogue record for this book is available from the
British Library.

Microsoft Press books are available through
booksellers and distributors worldwide. For further
information about international editions, contact your local
Microsoft Corporation office. Or contact Microsoft Press
International directly at fax (206) 936-7329.

Acquisitions Editor: Lucinda Rowley
Project Editor: John Pierce
Technical Contact: Kurt Meyer

FIELD GUIDE TO THE

INTERNET

Stephen L. Nelson

The Field Guide to the Internet is divided into four sections. These sections are designed to help you find the information you need quickly.

1 ENVIRONMENT

Terms and ideas you'll want to know to get the most out of the Internet. All the basic parts of Internet are shown and explained. The emphasis here is on quick answers, but most topics are cross-referenced so that you can find out more if you want to.

Diagrams of key Internet components, with quick definitions, cross-referenced to more complete information.

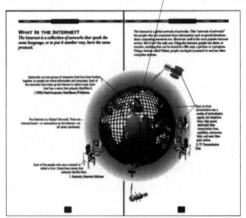

Tipmeister

Watch for me as you use this Field Guide. I'll point out helpful hints and let you know what to watch for.

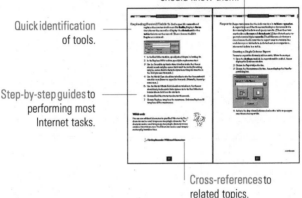

INTRODUCTION

••

In the field and on expedition, you need practical solutions. Fast. This Field Guide provides just these sorts of lightning-quick answers. But take two minutes now and read the introduction. It explains how this unusual little book works.

WHAT IS A FIELD GUIDE?

Sometime during grade school, my parents gave me a field guide to North American birds. With its visual approach, its maps, and its numerous illustrations, that guide delivered hours of enjoyment. The book also helped me better understand and more fully appreciate the birds in my neighborhood. And the small book fit neatly in a child's rucksack. But I'm getting off the track.

This book works in the same way as that field guide. It organizes information visually with numerous illustrations. And it does this in a way that helps you more easily understand and enjoy working with the Internet using a personal computer running Microsoft Windows 95. For new users, the Field Guide provides the essential information necessary to start using the Internet. But the Field Guide isn't only for beginners. For experienced users, the Field Guide provides concise, easy-to-find descriptions of Internet tasks, terms, and techniques.

WHEN YOU HAVE A QUESTION

Let me explain then how to find the information you need. You'll usually want to flip first to the Environment section, which is really a visual index. You find the picture that shows what you want to do or the task you have a question about. If you want to know how to connect to the Internet, you flip to pages 4 and 5, which talk about different ways you connect your personal computer to the Internet.

Next you read the captions that describe the parts of the picture. Say, for example, that you want to use an Internet access provider. On page 4, there's a caption that describes what Internet access providers are.

You'll notice that some captions use boldface terms or are followed by a little paw print and additional **boldface** terms. These refer to entries in the second section, Internet A to Z, and provide more information related to the caption's contents. (The paw print shows you how to track down the information you need. Get it?)

Internet A to Z is a dictionary of more than 200 entries that define terms and describe tasks. (After you've worked with the Internet a bit or if you're already an experienced user, you'll often be able to turn directly to this section.) So, if you have just read the caption that talks about Internet access providers, you'll see the term **PPP** in boldface, indicating a cross-reference. If you don't know what PPP is, you can flip to the PPP entry in Internet A to Z.

When an entry in Internet A to Z appears as a term within another entry, I'll **boldface** it the first time it appears in that entry. For example, as part of describing what PPP is, I might tell you that when you use a PPP, your PC becomes a **host computer** on the Internet for the duration of your connection. In this case, the words **host computer** appear in bold letters—alerting you to the presence of another entry explaining the term host computer. If you don't understand the term or want to do a bit of brushing up, you can flip to the entry for more information.

WHEN YOU HAVE A PROBLEM

The third section, Troubleshooting, describes problems that new and casual users of the Internet often encounter. Following each problem description, I list one or more solutions you can employ to fix the problem.

WHEN YOU WONDER ABOUT A COMMAND

The Quick Reference at the end of the Field Guide describes the **Internet Explorer, HyperTerminal, Microsoft Exchange,** and **Telnet** menu commands, as well as the **FTP** commands. (You enter the FTP commands using a command prompt.) If you want to know what a specific command does, turn to the Quick Reference. Don't forget about the Index either. You can look there to find all references in this book to any single topic.

CONVENTIONS USED HERE

I have developed three other conventions to make using this book easier for you. Rather than use wordy phrases such as "Activate the File menu and then choose the Print command" to describe how you choose a menu command, I'm just going to say, "Choose the File Print command."

Another thing. I've rather freely tossed out **uniform resource locators,** or URLs. And to make them stand out on the page, I've *italicized* them. OK, now I know that you might not know what these URL things are yet. But after you've noodled around a bit—and learned how to use them—you'll be happy I provided them. They give you the precise directions for finding cool stuff on the Internet.

Finally, when I give commands you type at a command prompt—such as in **UNIX** or using the **FTP** client—I *italicize* the command name.

ENVIRONMENT

Need to get the lay of the land quickly? Then the Environment is the place to start. It defines the key terms you'll need to know and the core ideas you should understand as you begin exploring the Internet.

WHAT IS THE INTERNET?

The Internet is a collection of networks that speak the same language, or to put it another way, use the same protocol.

Networks are just groups of computers that have been hooked together so people can share information and computers. Each of the networks that make up the Internet is called a domain. Each domain has a name that uniquely identifies it.

❧ DNS; Host Computer; Host Names; IP Address

The Internet is a Global Network. There are Internet hosts—or connections to the Internet—on all seven continents.

Each of the people who use a network is called a User. Users have names that uniquely identify them.

❧ Account; Internet Address

The Internet is a global network of networks. This "network of networks" lets people who are connected share information and, in special situations, share computing **resources** too. Electronic mail is the most popular Internet service. But it isn't the only one. Using the Internet, people can share, or transfer, anything that can be stored in a **file**: text, a picture, or a program. Using a feature called **Telnet**, people can **log in** (connect) to and use other computer systems.

Host-to-Host Connections use a variety of technologies: regular old telephone lines, high-speed, dedicated data-transmission lines, satellites, microwave links, and even fiber-optic cables.

T1 Transmission Line

CONNECTING TO THE INTERNET

To use any resource or service on the Internet, you first need to connect to it.

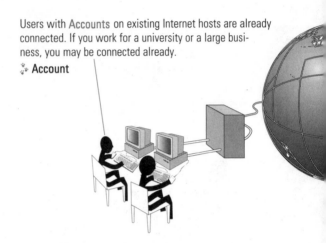

Users with Accounts on existing Internet hosts are already connected. If you work for a university or a large business, you may be connected already.

⁘ Account

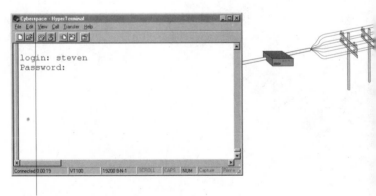

Internet access providers offer pay-for-use accounts on computers that are connected directly to the Internet. With a modem and a personal computer, you can often connect to a local access provider.

⁘ HyperTerminal; PPP; Shell Account; SLIP

People get connected in a variety of ways. The cheapest, easiest, and slowest-speed way to get connected is to get a **shell account** on another computer that is connected to the Internet. With the cheap, easy, slow way, you use your personal computer and **modem** to connect by way of an **access provider.** The most expensive, most complicated, and most powerful way to get connected, or "wired," is to have your network become one of the Internet's networks.

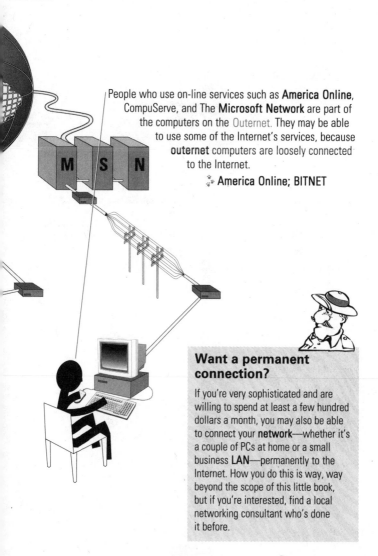

People who use on-line services such as **America Online,** CompuServe, and The **Microsoft Network** are part of the computers on the Outernet. They may be able to use some of the Internet's services, because **outernet** computers are loosely connected to the Internet.

⁂ **America Online; BITNET**

Want a permanent connection?

If you're very sophisticated and are willing to spend at least a few hundred dollars a month, you may also be able to connect your **network**—whether it's a couple of PCs at home or a small business **LAN**—permanently to the Internet. How you do this is way, way beyond the scope of this little book, but if you're interested, find a local networking consultant who's done it before.

SENDING ELECTRONIC MAIL

The Internet's most popular service is electronic mail, or e-mail.

E-Mail Programs let you create and send mail messages. Typically, they also let you read and organize mail messages others send you.

Addresses give the names of both the user and host.
❖ Domain Names; Internet Address

Interest Lists are electronic **mailing lists** of people who have a special interest in a specific topic. By joining an interest list—putting your name on the mailing list— you can see tons of messages related to a topic.
❖ FAQ; Lurk; Netiquette

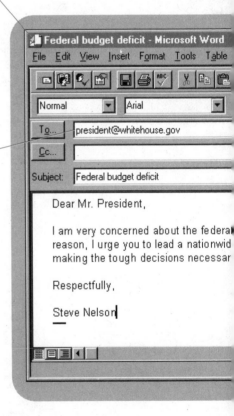

Federal budget deficit - Microsoft Word

File   Edit   View   Insert   Format   Tools   Table

Normal   Arial

To...   president@whitehouse.gov

Cc...

Subject: Federal budget deficit

Dear Mr. President,

I am very concerned about the federal
reason, I urge you to lead a nationwid
making the tough decisions necessar

Respectfully,

Steve Nelson

To send someone electronic mail, you create a mail message. The message includes the name and address of the person to whom the message should be delivered, the text of the message, and your name and address. Once you send your message, it is passed from **host** to host until the message reaches its destination.

Mail **gateways** connect the Internet to other networks such as **America Online,** CompuServe, GEnie, and MCI Mail, so you can send mail messages to users of these **outernet** services, too.

cit. For this
that focuses on
the budget.

How secure are e-mail messages?

It's not easy to intercept e-mail messages, and most people wouldn't intercept others' mail intentionally, but you should know it is possible to eavesdrop on e-mail messages. For this reason, some people encrypt messages.

Newsgroups

Newsgroups resemble interest lists. In newsgroups, mail messages are collected and organized by topic. The difference is that newsgroup mail messages, called **articles,** aren't distributed but are stored on central computers, called news **servers.** You decide which newsgroup articles you want to read—they aren't sent to you.

FILE AND HYPERTEXT TRANSFERS
File and hypertext transfers represent another way to share information on the Internet.

Data archives exist all over the world. Using the Internet, you should be able to access publicly accessible data archives.

Anonymous FTP; Netiquette

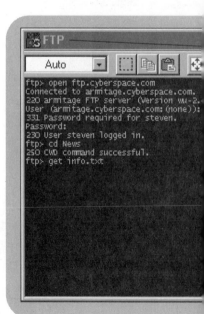

```
ftp> open ftp.cyberspace.com
Connected to armitage.cyberspace.com.
220 armitage FTP server (Version wu-2.
User (armitage.cyberspace.com:(none)):
331 Password required for steven.
Password:
230 User steven logged in.
ftp> cd News
250 CWD command successful.
ftp> get info.txt
```

Compression utilities shrink files so they take less time to transmit over the Internet. When you receive a file that has been compressed, you need to decompress ("unshrink") it.

PKZIP

File transfers let you copy files between Internet hosts. To transfer files between Internet hosts, you use the **FTP**, or file transfer protocol. You can copy almost anything that can be stored in a **file**: programs (for a variety of computers and operating systems), graphic images, and, of course, plain text files.

Hypertext transfers let you move graphic images, sound, and even video between Internet hosts. In fact, the hypertext transfer protocol—also known as **HTTP**—is what makes the **World Wide Web** possible.

⁂ FTP; GIF; Uniform Resource Locator

File location tools such as **Gopher, Archie,** and **World Wide Web** make it easier to find **files** you want—even if it means you need to search **hosts** all over the world.

20 16:06:58 PST 1994) ready.

File retrieval usually requires you to start a **client** like **FTP** or a **Web browser** like **Internet Explorer** and then to issue a command indicating that you want to get a file. To retrieve a file using FTP, you have to give the precise name of the file. To retrieve a file using Internet Explorer, you just click the file's name in a list.

⁂ Downloading Files

TELNETTING

The Internet also allows you to remotely connect, or log in, to other Internet hosts.

You use Telnet to connect to another Internet **host**. Once you connect to the other host, you log in by providing a username and a password.

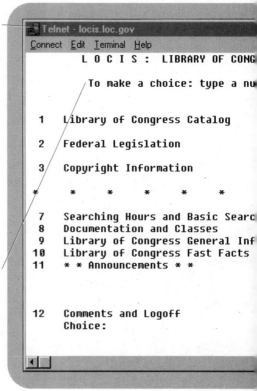

```
Telnet - locis.loc.gov
Connect  Edit  Terminal  Help
        L O C I S :  LIBRARY OF CONG

        To make a choice: type a nu

1    Library of Congress Catalog

2    Federal Legislation

3    Copyright Information

*      *      *      *      *      *

7    Searching Hours and Basic Searc
8    Documentation and Classes
9    Library of Congress General Inf
10   Library of Congress Fast Facts
11   * * Announcements * *


12   Comments and Logoff
     Choice:
```

Menu Systems usually appear once you successfully log in to the other Internet host. Menu systems guide you through the services you can use.

Once you've done this, you can use the other computer system—or at least the parts of it you're allowed to use. One important factor to keep in mind is that computers and networks operate in different environments. So things may look a bit different once you connect. For example, if you're used to working in Windows and you **Telnet** to a **UNIX** network, the screens and the commands will look different. If you've Telnetted to a different country, you may even see a different language.

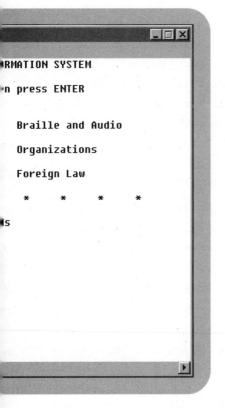

```
                                              _ □ ✕
▮RMATION SYSTEM

▸n press ENTER

    Braille and Audio

    Organizations

    Foreign Law

      *     *     *     *

▮s
```

Three Telnet tips

When you Telnet to another host, you should pay particular attention to three things: how you should disconnect once you're done, how to get help within the system, and the name and mail address of the person you should contact if a problem arises.

WORLD WIDE WEB

The World Wide Web is just a collection of multimedia documents that are connected by hypertext links.

Uniform Resource Locators are addresses that identify the locations of things like World Wide Web pages.
❖ **Uniform Resource Locator**

Graphic Images commonly appear in World Wide Web documents. Some graphic images are also hypertext links to graphic image files. You can view and **download** these files by clicking.
❖ **GIF; JPEG; Viewer**

Hypertext links connect different World Wide Web documents. Hypertext links are usually identified by boldfacing or color. To move to another document, you just click the hypertext link. Hypertext links can connect World Wide Web documents on different **hosts**.

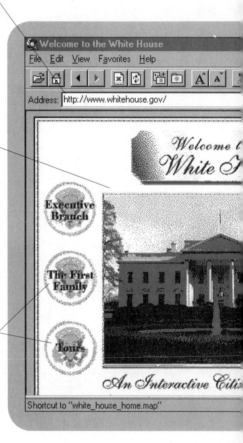

To view **World Wide Web** documents, you need a Web browser like
Internet Explorer and a **PPP** connection or an account on an
outernet online service that provides
World Wide Web browsing. To
move between World Wide Web
documents, you just click.

World Wide Web documents can
include text, pictures, and just about
anything else that can be stored in a
computer file.

Hypertext Transfers can be
very time-consuming—
especially when documents
include graphic images. To
alert you that a transfer is in
progress, Internet Explorer
flashes this logo.

Where do you start?

If you're new to the World
Wide Web, you need a
place to start exploring.
One good place to start is
http://www.yahoo.com. It
amounts to a directory of
World Wide Web pages
organized by category and
subcategory.

INTERNET A TO Z

Maybe it's not a jungle out there. But you'll still want to keep a survival kit close at hand. Internet A to Z, which starts on the next page, is just such a survival kit. It lists in alphabetic order the tools, terms, and techniques you'll need to know.

Access Provider   An access provider is a company that lets you connect to its Internet **host,** usually for a fee. Once you're connected, your computer works either like a temporary Internet host or like a "dumb terminal" on which you can use the Internet by means of your connection to the provider's **network.** (In other words, you use your keyboard and your monitor, but it's really the other computer and its software that you're using.) People who talk about the Internet being an "information superhighway" like to say that access providers are like on-ramps—they give you a way to get on the road.

One thing that's a little bit confusing but important to understand is that you pay an access provider merely to *access* the Internet. You're not paying anything to *use* the Internet. To go back to the on-ramps on the information superhighway analogy, access providers set up toll booths on the on-ramps so you can get on the highway. But you actually use the highway for free.

Let me give you a few tips on picking an access provider. First, check prices. You can pay anywhere from $10 to around $50 a month for an access provider's service. (To keep your costs down, you'll probably also want to choose a local access provider—to save on long-distance telephone charges.) Second, you should also verify that you'll be able to connect when you want. (You can test this just by trying to connect a few times before you actually sign up.) Finally, you probably want to verify that your access provider gives you access to the **resources** that interest you. (Some access providers don't give you access to the more controversial and sensational newsgroups, for example.) So ask about access to whatever you're interested in.

.•. **Connections; Outernet; Shell Account**

Account   You usually need an account to use big computer **networks** and systems, like those owned by universities or large businesses. As part of setting up your account, the system administrator gives you a **username** that you use to identify yourself to the system and a **password** so you can get into the system.

America Online   America Online is an **online service** that gives you access to a bunch of different stuff, including the Internet. However, I'm not going to describe how you do Internet stuff with America Online in this book.

I will say that if you want to **e-mail** someone who subscribes to America Online, you just need to tag the America Online **domain name**, *aol.com*, onto the end of his or her **username**. For example, if you want to send an e-mail message to me at my America Online address, you need to know my e-mail name, which is *StphnLNlsn,* and then you just put my e-mail name together with America Online's domain name to get my address:

StphnLNlsn@aol.com

🐾 **Netiquette; Outernet**

Anchor   The **hot links** in **World Wide Web** documents—the same ones you click to move from document to document—are sometimes called anchors. I don't really know why. But I don't make the rules.

Anonymous FTP

Anonymous FTP just means that someone without an **account** on an Internet **host** can still **FTP.** In other words, if an Internet host allows anonymous FTPs, you can connect to the host (no matter who you are) and start FTPing.

Using Anonymous FTP

To use anonymous FTP, you usually log on to another host by specifying your **username** as *anonymous* and your **password** as your **e-mail** address. For example, I would enter something along these lines:

```
username:   anonymous
password:   steven@cyberspace.com
```

You know what, though? There's something else you should know about anonymous FTP. And it's pretty important. Whoever owns and operates an anonymous FTP site is just doing it to be nice. It's their way of being good guys or gals, of performing a public service. You're not paying anything for this service. You're being given a free gift. So be gracious and grateful.

List of Useful Anonymous FTP Sites

There are a bunch of anonymous FTP sites. I can't list them all, but here's a starter list of **uniform resource locators (URLs)** that you can use to track down and explore some of the more popular and useful FTP sites for Windows 95 users:

Uniform resource locator	What the site offers
ftp://ftp.microsoft.com	Microsoft Corporation programs—such as those for Windows 95
ftp://ftp.ncsa.uiuc.edu	National Center for Supercomputing Applications stuff from the University of Illinois at Urbana-Champaign—such as the NCSA **Mosaic** Web **browser**
ftp://rtfm.mit.edu	**FAQs** maintained by the Massachusetts Institute of Technology on just about everything
ftp://ftp.cyberspace.com	Lots of Internet **clients** for the PC

Apple Macintosh   The computer world is divided into two camps, the Apple Macintosh camp and the PC camp. PC stands for "personal computer," and although Macintoshes are also personal computers, the term PC always refers to IBM computers and IBM compatibles.

This book focuses on connecting PCs that are running Windows 95 to the Internet. You won't find anything here specifically about Apple Macintosh computers, or "Macs" as they are called by their loyal users. But much of the stuff I say here also applies to Mac users.

Archie

Archie is a tool people use for finding **files** at **FTP** sites. In essence, what you do is tell Archie that you're interested in files with a specific name or files that have a specified string in their names (a string is just a chunk of text). Archie goes out and looks through a list of files at an Archie server. Then it builds a list of files (and their locations) that match your description and sends you the list. If you see something you want to retrieve, you use FTP to retrieve the file.

Using Archie with a Shell Account or a PPP or SLIP Connection

Windows 95 users have a couple of ways to use Archie. One method is to send an **e-mail** message to one of the Archie servers. To do this, just learn the **domain name** of an Archie server. For example, maybe you learn there's an Archie server named *archie.rutgers.edu.* (There actually is an Archie server with this domain name.) Once you have this information, send an e-mail message to Archie at the Archie server. For example, to send an e-mail to archie.rutgers.edu, you send the e-mail to *archie@archie.rutgers.edu.* Oh, one other thing. Your e-mail message needs to use the message text

```
find filename
```

The **file name** should be either the file name or a portion of the file name. For example, if you want to find files that use the word "mouse," your message text is

```
find mouse
```

A little while later—it could easily be an hour—you'll get back an e-mail message that lists files that use the word or string you

specified. What follows is actual text from the response to an Archie request I made by e-mail.

```
Host me10.lbl.gov   (128.3.128.110)
Last updated 15:54 15 May 1995

    Location: /pub/hp_X11R3_tape/poskbitmaps
      FILE   -r--r--r--    408 bytes  20:00   4 Apr 1989  mouse.xbm.Z

    Location: /pub/hp_X11R3_tape/poskbitmaps/dcm_cursors
      FILE   -r--r--r--    255 bytes  20:00   4 Apr 1989  cockmouse.xbm
      FILE   -r--r--r--    255 bytes  20:00   4 Apr 1989  deadmouse.xbm
      FILE   -r--r--r--    255 bytes  20:00   4 Apr 1989  diagmouse.xbm
      FILE   -r--r--r--    258 bytes  20:00   4 Apr 1989  mouse_icon.xbm
      FILE   -r--r--r--    255 bytes  20:00   4 Apr 1989  tinymouse.xbm
```

The host name with the files.

The directory.

Another method is simply to **Telnet** to an Archie server (**netiquette** says you should almost always use one that's close to your host), sign on using Archie as the username but without a password, and then use its commands. After you've Telnetted to the Archie server and you see the Archie command prompt, enter the find command:

```
find filename
```

There's more to Archie...

There's more to Archie than I've described here. You can use special Archie commands to specify whether the file name you're entering is the complete file name or just a portion of the file name. (The default, or usual, search method is to look for files that start with the filename parameter.) There are also commands that geographically limit the Archie servers that get searched. If you want more information, refer to one of the larger books about the Internet. *The Whole Internet Users Guide*, written by Ed Krol and published by O'Reilly and Associates, is one such book—and a great reference.

continues

Archie *(continued)*

Finding an Archie Server

You need to know an Archie server's domain name before you can send it e-mail or try to Telnet to it, of course. So here's a list of Archie servers that were active as I was writing this book:

Server	Location
archie.au	Australia
archie.edvz.uni-linz.ac.at	Austria
archie.univie.ac.at	Austria
archie.cs.mcgill.ca	Canada
archie.uqam.ca	Canada
archie.funet.fi	Finland
archie.univ-rennes1.fr	France
archie.th-darmstadt.de	Germany
archie.ac.il	Israel
archie.unipi.it	Italy
archie.wide.ad.jp	Japan
archie.hana.nm.kr	Korea
archie.sogang.ac.kr	Korea
archie.uninett.no	Norway
archie.rediris.es	Spain
archie.luth.se	Sweden
archie.switch.ch	Switzerland
archie.nctuccca.edu.tw	Taiwan
archie.ncu.edu.tw	Taiwan
archie.doc.ic.ac.uk	United Kingdom
archie.hensa.ac.uk	United Kingdom
archie.sura.net	USA (Maryland)
archie.unl.edu	USA (Nebraska)
archie.internic.net	USA (New Jersey)
archie.rutgers.edu	USA (New Jersey)
archie.ans.net	USA (New York)

Getting an up-to-date list of Archie servers

You can get a list of active Archie servers like the one shown above by including the *servers* command in an e-mail message you send to an Archie server. The *servers* command, like any Archie command, needs to be the first word and on its own line in the message text.

Using Archie with The Microsoft Network

The Microsoft Network doesn't provide direct connections to Archie servers. So to conduct an Archie search, you need to send an e-mail message to a nearby server. I describe how you do this in the preceding paragraphs under "Using Archie with a Shell Account or a PPP or SLIP Connection."

ARPA

ARPA is an acronym for Advance Research Project Agency. ARPA is the central research and development agency for the United States Department of Defense (DoD). You're wondering, of course, what any of this has to do with the Internet. Well, quite a lot actually. Over the past 20 years, ARPA funded a bunch of computer-related projects that shaped the computer industry and the Internet. BSD (Berkeley) **UNIX**, to take one example, and the **TCP/IP** protocol to take another. Most significant to our little discussion, however, is the fact that ARPA funded the ARPANET **network** that served as the starting point of the Internet.

 Gulf War

Article   People often call the messages that get posted to a **newsgroup** "articles." This name makes sense if you think of a newsgroup as an electronic newspaper or magazine. If newspapers and magazines contain articles, so too must newsgroups.

If people respond to an article by posting another article, the first article and its responses are called a **thread**.

Authentication   Authentication refers to the process by which an access provider's **host computer** makes sure that you and your computer are who you say you are. You can't just **log on** to an **access provider's** host computer. You have to provide your name or a **username**. And you need to provide a **password**.

By the way, making the **PPP** connection is a little easier if you're making a PPP connection to a host computer that supports one of the authentication **protocols**, PAP (Password Authentication Protocol) or CHAP (Challenge-Handshake Authentication Protocol). (Don't get bummed out by kooky protocol acronyms. I find them just as irritating as you do.) You can store your username and your password with the other Internet connection information. When Windows 95 logs on to the access provider's computer, it supplies your username and password. So you don't have to. If this is your situation, you don't need to tell Windows 95 to bring up a terminal after you make the PPP connection.

Backbone  NSFNET

Bandwidth
When people talk about the Internet, they use the term bandwidth to describe how much data can be transmitted in a given time, say a second. In these cases, people usually calibrate the bandwidth in **bits per second** (bps), Kilobits per second (Kbps), or Megabits per second (Mbps).

People who like big words use the term bandwidth to describe people who can absorb or transmit a bunch of information really quickly. (Ideally, then, you want to be a high-bandwidth person.)

T1 Transmission Lines; T3 Transmission Lines

Baud
Baud (rhymes with "Maude") is the measure of data-transmission speed. When it comes to **modem** speeds, people often talk about the "baud rate," although modem speed is not measured in bauds. Actually, modem speed is measured by the number of data bits that can be transmitted in a second. That is, modem speed is measured in **bits per second** (bps), Kilobits per second (Kbps), or Megabits per second (Mbps).

Modem

BBS

BBS is an acronym that stands for bulletin board system. In essence, BBSs work like those cork bulletin boards you see at the local grocery store. You know the ones I mean, right? The same ones where ancient Winnebagos are offered for sale, where 12-year-old kids offer baby-sitting services, and rewards are offered for lost dogs.

The only difference between cork bulletin boards and BBSs is that you post and read BBS messages electronically by using your computer and a **modem.** All you need is a communications program like Windows 95's **HyperTerminal** application to connect to a BBS. If you want to make a connection, the best approach is to just call the BBS operator and ask how you're supposed to make it.

By the way, BBSs aren't necessarily part of the Internet— although they can be. You do often see them being advertised slyly on the Internet, however. For example, some BBSs post graphics files and utilities in **newsgroups.** The BBS operators hope that once you see these newsgroups, you'll learn about their graphics files and utilities, and you'll pay big money to **download** them.

Bit

Bit stands for "binary digit." A bit is the amoeba of computer data. It is the smallest unit. Each bit represents a 1 or a 0. Bits are grouped in bunches of eight to form bytes, and bytes represent real information, such as letters and the digits 0 through 9. Modem transmission speeds, by the way, are measured in **bits per second.**

 Baud; Kilobyte

Bitmap

A bitmap is simply a pattern of colored dots. On your screen, each colored dot is created as a pixel of light and is described by one or more **bits** (binary digits). This sounds like a bunch of gobbledygook, but if the colored dots are arranged in the right way, you get a picture like the one shown below.

The reason I mention this is that you can **download** bitmap files in various file formats from newsgroups and FTP sites. Both **GIF** and **JPEG** formats are common, for example.

As a young man, I almost got the chance to shake President Kennedy's hand. But this other kid—I think his name was Bill— cut in front of me. And I lost my chance.

As a point of historical reference, I'll also mention that probably the best known bitmaps were those created in the late nineteenth century by the French impressionist Georges Seurat. In this case, however, the colored dots were created by brushstrokes on canvas rather than by pixels of light. And you thought this book was just about computers...

BITNET BITNET is an acronym—almost. It stands for "Because It's Time NETwork." BITNET started in the early 1980s and was mostly a university-oriented **network.** It networks mainly IBM and DEC mainframes and minicomputers. Usually used for mail and **file** transfers, BITNET's LISTSERV-based **mailing lists** are numerous and still very active. But today BITNET is diminishing in light of the Internet's popularity.

You don't really need to know anything about BITNET. But you sometimes hear the term being thrown around, so I thought, "What the heck," and decided to include this thumbnail sketch.

Bits Per Second Your computer and all the other computers connected to the Internet use **bits** (binary digits) to store information. If you could look at your hard disk with a disk viewing utility (and they do exist), you would see a bunch of 1s and 0s. As a practical matter, you don't really need to know anything about bits (or bytes either). But they are sort of relevant because **modem** speeds are described in bits per second, or bps. A 2,400 bps modem can theoretically spew or swallow a stream of slightly more than a couple thousand 1s and 0s every second. A 14,400 bps, or 14.4Kbps, modem can theoretically spew or swallow a stream of roughly fourteen thousand 1s and 0s every second. The faster the modem, the easier and faster it is to move data around the Internet. If you want to browse the **World Wide Web,** for example, you need a modem that goes at least 14.4Kbps.

⁘ **Baud**

BPS ⁘ **Bits Per Second**

Bridge You don't need to know the term bridge to use the Internet. But the term may come in handy at a cocktail party or a coffee klatch. A bridge is a device that connects two **networks** so they appear to be a single, larger network.

  Gateway

Browser A browser is a program that lets you look at **World Wide Web** documents. NCSA **Mosaic** is a browser, for example. And so is **Internet Explorer,** which comes with Microsoft Plus! for Windows 95. You now know everything you need to know to use the term browser with confidence. But since you're still reading, let me tell you a couple more things. Most browsers let you browse, or view, both the graphics and text components of World Wide Web documents. But there are also browsers that let you look at just the text. For example, if you have a **shell account** and your **access provider** supports the Lynx program, you can view just the text components of World Wide Web documents. (You might want to do this, for example, if your connection to the Internet is slow—say less than 28.8Kbps—or if you are really only interested in the text portions of the documents you are viewing.)

Byte Kilobyte

CERT   CERT is another acronym. It stands for Computer Emergency Response Team. Formed by the Advance Research Project Agency (**ARPA**) of the Department of Defense in 1988, CERT worries about the security of Internet hosts. So what does CERT do? CERT's main functions are to collect information about security breaches, coordinate responses to security breaches, and train the Internet community about security. It periodically issues advisories on security problems. You don't really need to know anything about CERT—just as you don't need to know anything about the U.S. Army's Delta Force Commandos. But it's reassuring to know that the CERT (and the Delta Force Commandos) exist.

If you're really interested in what CERT does...

For recent advisories, check the newsgroup *comp.security.announce*. Archives of old advisories, as well as security-related programs and information, can be found at *ftp://ftp.cert.org*.

Certs

You know what Certs are, right? They're those breath-mint candies that you pop into your mouth before you plant a kiss on your honey. Hubba, hubba.

☙ **CERT**

Circuit Switched Network

A circuit switched network is what the Internet isn't. Okay, that's sort of a goofy topic sentence. But let me explain. In a circuit switched network, each network connection requires a dedicated line—a wire, fiber-optic cable, even a satellite link or a microwave "link." The key feature of a circuit switched network is that when one computer is talking to another computer, whatever the computers are using to talk to each other is only used for their connection. The most common circuit switched network is the telephone system. When your computer (the one inside your skull) is talking with another computer (perhaps the one inside your boss's skull), the telephone line you're using is dedicated to your conversation and nothing else.

Now you might think that this has nothing to do with the Internet. And I guess you're right. But the reason I brought all this up is that knowing what a circuit switched network is helps you better understand what a **packet switched network** is, which is what the Internet uses.

Client

When you're talking about the Internet, a client is a software program running on your personal computer that lets you do Internet stuff. Windows 95 comes with several Internet clients, including **FTP, Ping,** and **Telnet.** If you have the Microsoft Plus! for Windows 95 software, you also have something called the **Internet Explorer,** which is a Web **browser** client. Client software programs work with server software programs that run on the computers you connect to.

☙ **Server**

Connections   There are a bunch of different ways to connect to
the Internet. The easiest and least expensive way is to get
a **shell account** from an **access provider.** If you choose
this route, you use a communications application like
HyperTerminal to connect to the access provider's **host
computer.** (Some people also call this connection method
a dial-up, or terminal emulation, account.) This Field
Guide, by the way, assumes that many of you are using
shell accounts for Internet connections. So I spend quite
a bit of time describing HyperTerminal and even some
UNIX programs, like **PINE** and **TIN,** that your access
provider is likely to give you.

A slightly more expensive and complicated method of
connecting to the Internet is with a **PPP** or **SLIP** connection. You have to use Windows 95's **Dial-Up Networking**
feature to make this sort of connection. And that means
you need to do a bit of fiddling. But PPP and SLIP accounts let you do more and do it faster. With a PPP or
SLIP account, for example, you can browse graphical
World Wide Web documents. This Field Guide assumes
that a whole bunch of readers will also use (or least be interested in) a PPP or SLIP connection. So I describe how
you go about setting up and making a PPP or SLIP connection and how you use the Internet clients that come
with Windows 95 for just such a purpose. Windows 95
comes with **Telnet, FTP,** and **Internet Explorer** (a Web
browser), as well as some other, less important utilities—
Ping, Route, and Tracert.

About the Internet Setup Wizard

When you install Plus! for Windows 95, the setup program asks
if you want to set up an Internet connection. If you indicate you
do, the Wizard walks you through the steps for setting up a PPP
connection.

One other common way to connect to the Internet is by first connecting to an **online service** such as The **Microsoft Network** and then using its Internet connections, or **gateways,** to connect to the Internet. I also think there's a pretty good chance that many readers use this connection method. (Windows 95 comes with The Microsoft Network software built right into the operating system. So all you have to do is sign up—something you can do by entering a handful of information into a window and clicking a few buttons.) Unfortunately, online services are difficult to cover in a book like this because they're changing all the time. (The Microsoft Network, for example, continues to add to its Internet capabilities all the time. And so do the other online services.) For this reason, I'll talk about this Internet connection method a little bit, but not as much.

I should probably point out that there are a handful of other online services that connect to the Internet. If you already subscribe to another online service—such as **America Online,** CompuServe, or Prodigy—you can connect to the Internet by using their gateways. While I don't describe the mechanics of using the gateways that these other online services provide, you'll still find much of what you read here useful and applicable.

What's more, if you had just scads of money, the time, and the technical expertise, you could connect your computer or **network** to the Internet permanently by using something like a **T1 transmission line.** I don't describe in this little book how you do this. I do want you to know that if you're going this route, I'm very envious of you.

Cybernaut   You're probably a cybernaut, my friend. Oh sure. Maybe you're still just getting your feet wet. But if you're using the Internet, you qualify as a cybernaut.

Cyberspace   Cyberspace is one of those loosely defined terms that—and this is very handy—most people use to mean whatever they want. If you put me on the spot and made me define it, however, I would say that cyberspace refers to the sum total of the activities and information on the world's computers, particularly the computers that are connected to the Internet or the **outernet.**

Just to clear up possible confusion, I'll also tell you that my access provider's **domain name** is cyberspace.com. So in many of the figures in this book , you'll see the word "cyberspace" used.

DARPA ⁂ **ARPA**

Desktop   The desktop is the background screen that appears beneath application windows.

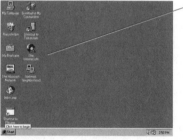

This background is the desktop.

What your desktop looks like depends on the desktop pattern you selected and the wallpaper you told Windows 95 to use to "paper over" the desktop pattern.

Dial-Up Networking

To connect to the Internet using the **PPP** or **SLIP** protocol, you need to already have a PPP or SLIP account set up with an **access provider**. And you need to use the Windows 95 Dial-Up Networking feature. You use Dial-Up Networking both to describe the connection (you do this only one time) and to make the PPP or SLIP connection (you do this every time you connect to the Internet). This business of setting up a PPP or SLIP account is probably one of the most tedious and complicated things you'll ever do in Windows 95, at least as far as the Internet goes. You need to add the **TCP/IP** protocol, configure a **domain name** server, bind the Dial-Up Network adapter to the TCP/IP protocol, and then set up a Dial-Up Networking connection.

Fortunately, you usually shouldn't have to deal directly with the Dial-Up Networking feature. When you install Microsoft Plus! for Windows 95, you indicate whether you want the Internet Jumpstart Kit installed. If you do, Windows 95 starts the Internet Setup Wizard. It walks you through the steps for adding the TCP/IP protocol, configuring the domain name server, binding the Dial-Up Network adapter, and then describing the Dial-Up Networking **connection.** The Internet Setup Wizard also adds a **shortcut icon** to the **desktop** for the **Internet Explorer.** So all you need to do to connect to your access provider and begin browsing the **World Wide Web** is double-click the shortcut icon. And if you use one of the other Internet **clients** that come with Windows 95—like FTP or Telnet—the client software also connects to your access provider automatically.

continues

Dial-Up Networking *(continued)*

Making a PPP or SLIP Connection Manually

If you need to make a PPP or SLIP connection manually, you can do that, too. Open the Dial-Up Networking folder and double-click on the connection. This tells Windows 95 to make the PPP or SLIP connection.

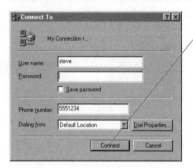

Windows 95 first displays the Connect To dialog box. You don't need to do anything with this dialog box. Just click Connect.

As Windows 95 makes the connection, it displays a dialog box that describes its progress.

After Windows 95 makes the connection—and this will take a few seconds—it displays a terminal window. You'll use this window to log on to the access provider's host.

Once you've logged on—and done anything else you do as part of logging on, such as identifying the terminal emulation you're using or invoking the PPP or SLIP connection with a command—you click the Continue command button. When the PPP or SLIP connection is successfully made, you see another dialog box that says you're connected. Your computer is now an Internet **host**. Welcome to the big leagues.

 Authentication

D

Document Cache Web browsers like **Internet Explorer** use
something called a document cache. The document cache
stores copies of **World Wide Web** documents on your
hard disk so you don't have to grab them from some distant World Wide Web **server** to read them. By default,
Internet Explorer uses up to 10 percent of your hard disk
for caching. You can change this percentage, however, by
choosing the Internet Explorer's View Options command, clicking on the Advanced tab, and then moving
the Cache slider button.

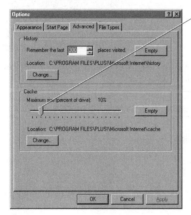

Drag this slider button to
change the cache size.

If you don't want to use cached documents

If you don't want to use cached documents, click the Refresh tool or choose the
View Refresh command. This tells Internet Explorer to grab a new copy of the
document from its World Wide Web server rather than use the cached copy of the
document on your hard disk.

Domain Names
The domain name identifies the organization that owns and operates an Internet network. The domain name has the format *organization.type*. The organization part is usually the name or acronym of the organization. For example *microsoft.com* or *mit.edu*. And organizations have to register their domain with **InterNIC**. The type part of the domain name can be one of the following:

Type	What it means
com	A company or commercial organization. For example, Microsoft's domain name is *microsoft.com*.
edu	An educational institution. For example, the Massachusetts Institute of Technology's domain name is *mit.edu*.
gov	A government site. For example, NASA's domain name is *nasa.gov*.
mil	A military site. For example, the United States Air Force's domain name is *af.mil*.
net	A gateway or other administrative host for a network. For example, UUNET's domain name is *uu.net*.
org	An organization that doesn't fit in the other classes of domain types. For example, the Electronic Frontier Foundation's domain name is *eff.org*.

Country Types
The domain names of organizations located outside of the United States use a two-letter country code either in place of or in addition to the three-letter organization-type codes just listed. For example, the two-letter country code for Australia is *au*. And the two-letter country code for Greece is *gr*.

Domain Name Service

Domain name service, or DNS, is like a smart, electronic post office. Imagine if all you had to do whenever you wanted to send someone a letter was write the person's name on the outside of the envelope. Then, down at the post office, some friendly postal worker looked up the address of the person and mailed the letter. Sounds nice, right? Well, that is basically what DNS does. Because of DNS, you can refer to a host by using its **host name.** DNS then does the work of looking up the host's **IP address** for you.

For example, if you wanted to fiddle-faddle around with the host named *ftp.microsoft.com*, the **TCP/IP** application you're using would use DNS to look up the correct IP address, which just happens to be 198.105.232.1. (Your machine or a machine you have access to must be configured to use a name **server** that performs the actual looking up.)

Downloading Files

How you move a **file** from the Internet to your PC depends on the way you've connected to the Internet. If you've connected with a **shell account** and you want to move a file from your **access provider's** computer to your PC, you use a communications application like **HyperTerminal.** If you've connected with a **PPP** or **SLIP** connection, you can move the file by using Windows 95's **FTP** client. If you're using an **online service** like The **Microsoft Network,** you use whatever commands the online service's client software provides.

⁘ Uploading Files

Emoticons ❖ Smileys

E-Mail   E-mail, or electronic mail, is the Internet's most popular
feature. If you have an e-mail client program and access
to an e-mail service, you can send electronic mail to just
about anyone whose e-mail address you know—the
president of the United States (e-mail name:
president@whitehouse.gov), me (e-mail name:
steven@cyberspace.com), and any of your friends or family
who are wired. (I don't know these people's e-mail addresses. So you need to call them and ask.)

By the way, Windows 95 comes with an Internet mail client. To use it, you start **Microsoft Exchange.** You also use
Microsoft Exchange for sending and receiving e-mail
from The **Microsoft Network.**

What's an e-mail message?

E-mail messages usually include just text. But they can include binary files—such
as graphic images and programs—as long as the e-mail **client** and **server** programs support something called **MIME**. What's more, **newsgroups** and **mailing
lists** (popular Internet features) are basically extensions of e-mail.

❖ **Microsoft Exchange; Microsoft Network; Pine**

E-Mail Lists ⁂ Mailing Lists

Encoded Files

Encoded Files Here's one of the weird aspects of Internet **newsgroups:** You can't post binary **files,** such as **bitmap** images or programs. You can post only text. If you know much about Internet newsgroups, however, you're shaking your head now. You already know that bitmap images and programs are two of the things that people post most often.

So what gives? Well, here's the weirdness: To post a binary file—such as a picture or program—the poster first turns the binary file into a text file. Binary-to-text conversion is called encoding, or uuencoding. When someone wants to **download** an encoded binary file, they need to turn the text file back into a binary file. Text-to-binary conversion is called decoding, or unencoding.

See all this gibberish? This is an encoded binary file.

Encoding Binary Files

You encode binary files before you post them by using an encoding/decoding utility. There are a bunch of these. I recently downloaded a shareware encoding/decoding utility called WINCODE from a newsgroup named *alt.binaries.utilities.* Once you've encoded a binary file and it has become a text file, you can post it to a newsgroup the same way you post any message.

continues

Encoded Files *(continued)*

Decoding, or Unencoding, Binary Files

You decode, or unencode, binary files either when you retrieve them with your newsgroup reader or when you move them to your PC with an encoding/decoding utility like WINCODE.

⁘ TIN; Troubleshooting: You Can't Decode a Binary File

Encryption When you encrypt something—like an e-mail message—it just means that you scramble the information so it can't be read by anyone who doesn't know how to unscramble it. When the recipient gets your e-mail message, he or she decrypts, or unscrambles, it in order to read it.

Mechanically, encryption is pretty simple. Let's take the following message as an example:

```
I'm dating Bob's mother but don't tell Bob!
```

If I create a simple little code that, for example, substitutes the number *2* for the letter *b*, fills spaces with the letter *x*, and substitutes the dollar sign for the letter *o*, the preceding message gets encrypted into this:

```
I'mxdatingx2$2'sxm$therx2utxd$n'txtellx2$2!
```

See how even a simple code makes a message pretty illegible? If Bob gets or intercepts this message, he probably wouldn't stumble onto my secret. But if my intended recipient knows the encryption scheme and can apply it backwards, he or she can easily decrypt and then read my message.

Anyone who really wanted to could probably figure out my simple code in relatively short order. But with a computer you can create and use wickedly complex encryption rules. In fact, with a computer's help, you can create and use encryption rules that are practically unbreakable.

So how does all of this apply to the Internet? While encryption may seem like something of interest to only the truly paranoid and to conspiracy theorists, actually it's not. Encryption is necessary for the Internet to become a truly commercial network. You wouldn't want to send your credit card number without encryption, for example. Without encryption, some miscreant might intercept your credit card number and charge a trip to Acapulco.

PGP; Pirates; ROT13

Escape Characters

If you connect to another Internet host—say you've just **Telnetted** to the host—you need a way to disconnect when you're done. The way you disconnect is by pressing an escape character. The escape character is probably a two-character key sequence that you type to signal you want to disconnect.

```
cyberspace/home/steven> telnet locis.loc.gov
Trying 140.147.254.3 ...
Connected to locis.loc.gov.
Escape character is '^]'.
```

When you connect to the U.S. Library of Congress's Telnet site, for example, you're told, among other things, that the escape character is ^]. The caret symbol (^) signifies the Ctrl key. So to disconnect from the Library of Congress's Telnet site, you press Ctrl+].

Typically, you get a bunch of information when you first connect to a host, and buried in that information is the escape character. Be sure to write the escape character down. Or, failing that, try some of the more common escape sequences—such as Ctrl+] or Ctrl+C.

continues

Escape Characters *(continued)*

Want to Telnet to the Library of Congress?

To Telnet to the Library of Congress, you just need to know the Telnet site name, which is *locis.loc.gov*. If you are using an **access provider's** Telnet feature or the Windows 95 Telnet command, you type *telnet locis.loc.gov* at the command prompt to get the locis system. If you are using a Web **browser** like Microsoft's **Internet Explorer**, you use the **uniform resource locator**: *telnet://locis.loc.gov.* Once you connect to the Library of Congress or to any other Telnet site, you use the site's menus to navigate and use the system.

Ethernet   Ethernet is a hardware standard for **LANs** developed by Xerox. It is one of the most popular standards. Ethernet can transfer data at speeds up to 10Mbps. So that's pretty cool. But you must have an Ethernet adapter for your PC to connect to an Ethernet-based **LAN**.

Let me see if there's anything else I can say about Ethernet... Well, as long as we're on the subject, I may as well tell you that there are three ways to make the actual connection based on the adapter and **network**: Thin Ethernet cable using a BNC connector, twisted pair or 10BASE-T cable using an RJ-45 connector, and Thick Ethernet cable using an AUI connector.

Oh, one other thing. Although Ethernet is pretty fast, its **bandwidth** is not fast enough for future multimedia applications. For that reason, a new protocol called Fast-Ethernet is under development that will allow speeds up to 100Mbps.

🐾 **Bits Per Second**

FAQ

FAQ is an acronym for Frequently Asked Questions. A FAQ is a compilation of questions and answers posted often on **newsgroups** and **mailing lists**. FAQs do a couple of things. They give you a feel for what a newsgroup or mailing list is about, and they keep questions that have already been answered many times from appearing yet again.

You probably should read the FAQ for a newsgroup or mailing list you're interested in. Unless you're someone who enjoys being the subject of nasty criticism and endless **flames**, you should definitely check a group's FAQ before you post.

Just the FAQs, ma'am

FAQs are posted regularly in newsgroups as well as on *news:// news.answers*. Archives of almost all FAQs can be found at *ftp:// rtfm.mit.edu/pub/usenet*. A good search form can be found at *http:/ /www.cis.ohio-state.edu/hypertext/faq/usenet/top.html*.

 Netiquette

File

In Computerland, you work with files. Data gets stored in files. Applications, or programs, are stored in files. When you begin work, you open a file. When you're done, you save and close it.

One of the main tasks the Internet performs, of course, is moving these files around. And, in fact, there's a protocol you'll probably work with that was created for the express purpose of moving files between Internet hosts: **FTP**.

File Extensions In MS-DOS and the earlier versions of Windows, you stuck a three-letter file extension at the end of **file names.** The file extension identified the file type. Because of this history, many of the **files** you **download** from the Internet use a file extension to identify the file type.

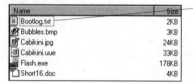

The three-letter string following the period is the file extension.

What's more, because of this history, it's considered good manners to **upload** files that follow the MS-DOS file naming conventions and use the three-letter file extension. Just so you know what some of the common file extensions identify, I've listed the common ones in the table that follows:

File extension	Type of file
ARC	A compressed file that's been scrunched with the archive utility.
EXE	A program, or executable, file.
GIF	A **bitmap** file that uses the Graphics Image Format, or **GIF.**
JPG	A bitmap file that uses the Joint Photography Experts Group, or **JPEG,** format.
MPG	A video that uses the Moving Pictures Experts Group, or **MPEG,** format.
TXT	A text file.
UUE	A binary file—such as a program or bitmap file—that's been turned into text using an Uuencode utility. To turn this file back into a program or bitmap file, you'll need to decode, or unencode, it.
ZIP	A file that's been compressed, or scrunched, using the **PKZIP** utility.

File Names

With Windows 95, you don't really have to worry about file names and **file extensions.** For all practical purposes, you can use as many characters as you want in a file name. And what's more, you don't have to worry about the file extension because Windows 95 takes care of that.

But things are a bit different on the Internet. Because of the legacy of MS-DOS's file-naming limitations and conventions, you should limit the names of the files you upload to eight characters. All numbers and letters that appear on your keyboard are okay to use in file names. And so are many other characters. You shouldn't, however, use characters that MS-DOS expects to use in special ways on its command line. These forbidden characters include spaces, asterisks, and question marks. You'll also want to use the file extension to identify the file format.

Naming a File

You usually give a file its file name when you choose the application's File Save As command.

File Pane

When you start the **Windows Explorer,** Windows displays a document window that shows the stuff that's connected to your computer—including any **folders** and **files.** This window is split into two chunks that I'm calling panes.

Since the right pane is the only one that shows files, I decided to call it the file pane. I should say that this is just something I made up. I don't think you'll see this term any place else, but if you do, tell them "Steve Nelson was here."

Finger   People with **shell accounts** usually have a special command available, called finger. (To be precise, this command is actually a **client** that runs on the **access
provider's** computer.) Here's the scoop. If you know
someone's e-mail name and the **domain name** of the **host**
they use, you might be able to learn their true identity by
fingering them. For example, say you've just gotten a
message from someone named "nelson" at *uxx.edu*.
Perhaps, before you reply, you want to learn a bit more
about this person. So you finger them. To do this, type
the command *finger* at the command prompt, followed
by the person's e-mail address. For example, to learn the
true identify of *nelson@uxx.edu*, you would type:

```
cyberspace/steven>finger nelson@uxx.edu
```

Assuming the host you've fingered responds (and it may
not), what you'll see next is some information on the certain someone you fingered, such as that shown here:

```
[uxx.edu]
        Name:  Nelson, Peter C.
   Department:  Electrical Engineering
        Title:  Assistant Professor
        Phone:  555-3210
          Fax:  555-1234
      Address:  3015 ERF
            :  Campus MC 154
    E-mail to:  Peter.C.Nelson@uxx.edu
  ADN Account:  nelson@xxx.uxx.edu
```

Flame
A flame is an **e-mail** message that's mean and nasty. If you e-mail a message to me and say that I'm a complete moron, utterly incapable of constructing a sentence, for example, that's a flame. By the way, if I e-mail you back a message that says your mother wears army boots and your sister is ugly, what we've got going is a "flame war."

Flames, as you might guess, violate all the rules of Internet good manners and etiquette. But because some of the people out surfing the Internet have the maturity of a grade schooler, you'll see quite a few flames. On a philosophical note, I suspect that the anonymity of the Internet has something to do with this meanness. You can say something really mean and threatening on the Internet, but you don't have to see the person's face or run into them at the grocery store.

⁙ **Netiquette; Spam**

Folder
Windows 95 uses folders to organize your disks and the **files** they store. (Folders, by the way, replace MS-DOS's directories.) You can also organize the files in a folder by creating folders within a folder. Basically, folders work like the drawers in a filing cabinet.

You can create folders and see how your disk is organized into folders by using **Windows Explorer.**

⁙ **Subfolder**

Folder Pane
I'm using the term folder pane to refer to the left half of the window that **Windows Explorer** displays to show you what's connected to your computer, how your disks' **folders** are organized, and which **files** are in the active folder. Because The **Microsoft Network** also uses the Windows Explorer interface, I'll also use the term folder pane when discussing The Microsoft Network.

Freenet The term freenet refers to an Internet **host** that people can use for free and thereby connect to the Internet for free. Schools, community groups, and libraries are often providers of freenet sites. If you're interested in exploring this angle, you might want to make telephone calls to schools, community groups, and libraries in your town.

On the subject of freenet sites, the downtown public library where I live (Seattle) provides a freenet site, and it has become popular with a bunch of homeless men. These guys, who call themselves the "network geeks," spend their considerable free time surfing the Internet from the library's freenet site. As one of the network geeks explained, "We're homeless but we're not stupid."

Free Speech You bought this book to learn more about the mechanics and the technology of the Internet. I know that. But I want to digress for just a moment and talk about free speech and the Internet.

The Internet, as you might know, makes it possible to share one's thoughts and ideas with millions of people. While this power isn't all that remarkable—after all, television and some of the big newspapers do it on a daily basis—it is remarkable in that there's no obligatory censorship or filtering of the information.

Think about it for a minute. Nowhere else can someone share a thought or idea with millions of people freely, without the help of editors, journalists, and media executives. That's the "good news," so to speak. But there's a "bad news" element to this lack of informal censorship and filtering. And it's the flip side of the same coin. Someone—anyone with an Internet connection—can share a thought or idea with millions of people freely. And in any group of 20 million people, of course, you'll find a few goofballs, dingbats, and dirtballs.

F

I strongly believe the good news outweighs the bad news. And I think you will too, if you think about it for a minute or so. But I need to warn you: Because some editor or journalist isn't filtering information for you, you need to filter the information for yourself. And because the Internet community is culturally diverse, you will most assuredly find material you disagree with on any subject about which you feel strongly. Politics. Religion. Sexuality. Good grammar.

I'm not going to spend a bunch more space on this. But I encourage you to respect and appreciate the enormous benefits of the Internet's contribution to free speech.

Bad news for movie makers, novelists, and conspiracy theorists

Jeepers, because we're on the subject, I should also mention that this communication change is bad news for some movie makers, novelists, and conspiracy theorists. A fundamental element of many thriller stories and conspiracy theories is a protagonist who has important information but can't share it with anybody important. Note, however, that with the Internet, this idea is totally outdated. In fact, by my rough calculation, more than a few of Alfred Hitchcock's movies, some of Robert Ludlum's novels, and most conspiracy theories become impossibly farfetched in light of this radical change in communication. If you have hard evidence that some world leader is a criminal, for example, you can post the evidence to an Internet **newsgroup** today and probably topple a government tomorrow. If you discover a cheap, renewable, safe energy source some Friday afternoon, you can tell the world about it over the weekend, and no one—not even somebody or some organization with billions or trillions of dollars to lose—can stop you.

FTP

FTP stands for file transfer protocol or file transfer program. Something like that. But that's not important. What is important is what FTP allows you to do. FTP allows you to move **files** from one Internet **host** to another. In fact, some hosts are set up specifically so you can rummage around inside them and look for stuff to FTP back to your host. (Your host can be either your access provider's computer or your own PC.) These hosts are called, not surprisingly, FTP sites. If any Joe or Jane can log on to an FTP site—and there are plenty of sites they can log on to—the FTP site is called an **anonymous FTP site.**

FTPing with an Access Provider

To FTP with a **shell account,** first log on to the **access provider's** network. You'll probably do this with a communications application like **HyperTerminal.** Once you're connected to the access provider, you can probably just type the command name *ftp* and the FTP site name at the command prompt.

To see how this works, let's say you want to get information about all the different mailing lists you can subscribe to and someone has told you there's a master list of this information at an FTP site called *ftp://rtfm.mit.edu/pub/usenet/news.answers/mail/mailing-lists.* Here's what you do to get the information:

1 Type *ftp rtfm.mit.edu* at the command prompt. This tells your access provider's host that you want to log in to the anonymous FTP site named *rtfm.mit.edu.* A few seconds will go by. Then you'll get a login prompt for the FTP site.

2 When prompted, enter your name, or **username,** as *anonymous.* Press Enter.

3 When prompted, enter your complete e-mail name as the **password.** (For example, I would enter *steven@cyberspace.com.*) Then you press Enter again. You'll next see the FTP host's logon screen, as shown on the following page:

```
cyberspace/home/steven> ftp rtfm.mit.edu
Connected to rtfm.mit.edu.
220 rtfm ftpd (wu-2.4(26) with built-in ls); bugs to ftp-bugs@rtfm.mit.edu
Name (rtfm.mit.edu:steven): anonymous
331 Guest login ok, send your complete e-mail address as password.
Password:
```

4 Change to the directory where the mailing list information is stored. You do this by typing the command *cd* followed by the complete path name of the directory with the stuff you want. In our little example, you would type *cd /pub/usenet/news.answers/ mail/mailing-lists*.

5 Display a list of the files in the directory. You can do this by typing the list command, *ls*, at the FTP prompt. (If you want the files listed in a single column, type the command *ls -1*.)

```
ftp> cd /pub/usenet/news.answers/mail/mailing-lists
250 CWD command successful.
ftp> ls
200 PORT command successful.
150 Opening ASCII mode data connection for file list.
part1
part01
part02
part03
part04
part05
part06
part07
part08
part10
part11
part12
part13
part14
part09
226 Transfer complete.
119 bytes received in 0.0079 seconds (15 Kbytes/s)
```

6 To retrieve one of the files, type the command *get* followed by the **file name**. To get the file named part01, for example, you would type *get part01*. You'll see a message that tells you the FTP resource is opening an ASCII data mode connection. Then you'll see some other stuff, including the length of time the transmission took.

7 To disconnect from the anonymous FTP site, type *disconnect*. You'll probably see a good-bye message.

8 To leave the FTP resource, type *quit*.

9 Once you have the file or files you want, you can download them in the usual way. For example, you can type the *sz* command, which tells the access provider to send the files using the **Zmodem** protocol. (There's more information on downloading files this way in the **HyperTerminal** entry.)

continues

FTP *(continued)*

Starting an FTP Session with a PPP or SLIP Connection

To start an FTP session with a **PPP** or **SLIP** connection, first start the FTP **client**. You can do this by following these steps:

1 Start Windows Explorer by clicking the Start button and then choosing Programs and Windows Explorer.

2 Display the contents of the Windows **folder**. (Depending on how your system is set up, the folder may be named something other than "Windows." In that case, just substitute the correct name in the following instructions.) One way to do this is by scrolling through the **folder pane** and then double-clicking on the Windows folder.

3 Open the FTP program. One way to do this is by scrolling through the **file pane** and then double-clicking on the FTP program. Once you've opened the FTP program, you'll see the FTP window in the middle of the Windows **desktop**.

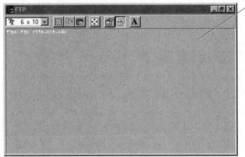

This is the FTP window.

4 If you've not already made your PPP or SLIP connection, Windows 95 will start **Dial-Up Networking** as soon as you try to connect to another host.

If you FTP often...

If you FTP often, set up a **shortcut icon** for the FTP program. A shortcut icon makes it much easier to start the FTP client. With a shortcut icon—it will appear on the **desktop**—all you do is double-click the icon to start the FTP client.

F

Want a complete list of the FTP client's commands?

The FTP client provides a bunch of different commands. And I describe them all in the "Quick Reference" section at the end of this book. In this entry, I only give you instructions on using the most common of these commands.

Connecting to an FTP Site with Windows 95's FTP Client

To connect to an FTP site, type the command *open* followed by the name of the FTP site.

For example, to connect to the anonymous FTP site rtfm.mit.edu, type *open rtfm.mit.edu*.

Once you connect, you'll be prompted for your username and a password. If the host is an anonymous FTP site, enter your username as *anonymous*. Enter your password as your e-mail address (including both your username and the domain name).

continues

FTP *(continued)*

Retrieving Files with Windows 95's FTP Client

Finding files using FTP is tough. In fact, it's basically for this reason that Internet clients such as **Archie,** Jughead, and Veronica were developed. If you don't know what you're looking for, try using one of those file-finding utilities.

Once you do find the file you're looking for, it's easy to retrieve it. Just type the *get* command followed by the file name. The FTP client will move the file from the FTP site to your host. For example, to get a file named Part01 at *rtfm.mit.edu*, you would type the following:

```
get Part01
```

Disconnecting from an FTP Site with Windows 95's FTP Client

To disconnect from an FTP site, just type the command *disconnect* at the command prompt. You'll see some messages, including one that says you've disconnected. If you want to connect to another FTP site, you can. Just follow the instructions provided in the earlier blurb about connecting to an FTP site with Windows 95's FTP client. If you want to end the FTP session, type the command *quit.*

Gopher; Internet Explorer; Troubleshooting: FTP; Quick Reference: FTP Client Commands

Gateway

A gateway is just a computer that connects an **IP** network and a non-IP network. You can look up the term IP in this book, but in case you need to know right away I'll tell you that IP stands for "internet protocol" and that an IP network is one that uses the internet protocol. For example, **online services** like **America Online,** CompuServe, The **Microsoft Network**, and Prodigy use gateways to connect to the Internet.

Bridge; Outernet

GIF

A GIF file is a bitmap file that uses the Graphics Image Format (GIF) file format. There's an ongoing argument about whether GIF files look better than the usual substitute, **JPEG** files. Some people swear that GIFs look better and that anyone who uploads anything else is either a simpleton or a jerk. The truth, however, is that high-quality JPEG files look just as good as high-quality GIF files. What's more, JPEG files are smaller and, therefore, a lot quicker to upload and download. To look at a GIF file, you need to have a **viewer** such as **Internet Explorer.**

Downloading Files

Gigabyte

A gigabyte is roughly 1,000 **megabytes.** Since a megabyte is roughly 1,000 **kilobytes,** it follows that a gigabyte is roughly 1,000,000 kilobytes. That's big. Really big. For example, with a 14.4Kbps **modem** spewing data at a rate of 14.4Kbps, it would probably take about a week to download a gigabyte of stuff.

Nits on bits

In the preceding paragraph, I only gave rough descriptions of the terms megabyte and gigabyte. To be painstakingly precise, a megabyte is actually 1,024 kilobytes, and a gigabyte is actually 1,024 megabytes or 1,048,576 kilobytes.

Gopher The great thing about the Internet is all the information it provides, but there's a problem with this. You need a way to sift through everything. You need a way to find the specific piece of data you want. You need, well, you need Gopher.

What's Gopher? Gopher is, in essence, a menu of Internet **resources.** These menus are maintained by Gopher servers. (The stuff that appears on Gopher menus is collectively called "Gopherspace.")

Understanding Gopher

To use Gopher, you just connect to a Gopher **server**. Then you begin choosing menu options. Ideally, you narrow the range of topics as you choose menu options, and then you find the topic you want.

Typically, Gopher servers emphasize a particular information category. Agricultural research. Federal law. Stuff like that. No matter which Gopher server you connect to, some of the menu options you see are, in essence, connections to other Gopher servers.

If I connect to the University of Minnesota Gopher server, this is what I see.

To search for information, I just start selecting menu options. Ultimately, I will connect to an Internet **resource** such as a **file** you can **FTP** or to a **Telnet** site.

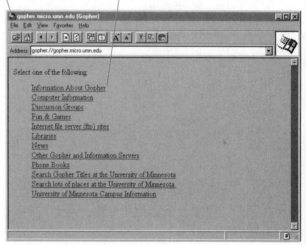

Connecting to a Gopher

How you connect to Gopher depends on whether you're using a **shell account** or a **PPP** or **SLIP** connection. If you're using a shell account, you need to ask your access provider for instructions. You may just be able to type *Gopher* at the command prompt, for example. Or, there may be a menu option on the access provider's main menu for connecting to a Gopher server.

If you're using a PPP or SLIP connection and **Internet Explorer,** you need to make your connection and start Internet Explorer. Then, you enter the **uniform resource locator** for the Gopher server into the Address drop-down list box. (If this is a Gopher server that you'll want to connect to frequently, you may want to add the URL to your favorite places list.)

Using Gopher

Once you've connected to a Gopher server, you start choosing menu options. If you connect to a Gopher server that itself catalogs information of the kind you're looking for, you may be able to find what you're looking for rather quickly (keep your fingers crossed).

Once you find that bit of information you're interested in, select it. If you're using a shell account's Gopher client, you may do this with a menu. If you're using Internet Explorer, click on the resource. Gopher downloads the file either to the access provider's computer (if you're using a shell account) or to your computer (if you're using a PPP or SLIP connection). If the Gopher client knows which application opens the file, it will even open the file for you. In the case of text files, Internet Explorer—acting as your Gopher client—tells **WordPad** to open the text file. (If you want to save a document you've retrieved with Gopher, you typically tell the application that opened the file to save it. For example, if WordPad opens a text file you've downloaded, you tell WordPad to save it.)

continues

Gopher *(continued)*

Finding Resources with Searchable Indexes

To make it easier to find resources, Gopher provides three search tools: searchable indexes, Veronica, and Jughead. I'll describe searchable indexes first. In the next two sections, I'll describe how to use Veronica and Jughead.

Okay, here's the deal on searchable indexes. Some of the menu options Gopher presents aren't really menu options at all. At least not in the regular sense. When you choose one of these menu options, called searchable indexes, what you are really telling the Gopher server is that you want specific information about the resources it catalogs.

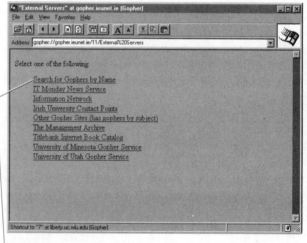

This menu option represents a searchable index. When you choose a searchable index, Gopher displays a dialog box.

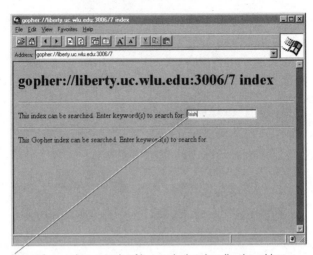

Enter a keyword or a couple of keywords that describe the subject you're interested in. A friend in Europe told me that authors don't pay any income tax in Ireland. So here I am starting my search for information on Ireland.

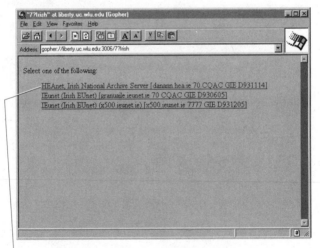

Here is the topic list I found using the keyword "Irish."

continues

Gopher *(continued)*

Finding Resources with Veronica

If you think about it for a minute, there's a problem with searchable indexes. They only look at an index of stuff for a Gopher directory. That means if you want to look in a bunch of different places, you have to search a bunch of searchable indexes. So how do you find the Gopher server or directory in the first place? You use Veronica. Veronica searches Gopher servers and Gopher directories. If it can find a server or directory associated with a keyword or keywords that you specify in your search, it lets you know.

Mechanically, using Veronica is like using a regular old searchable index. The only difference is that rather than choosing a Gopher menu option that describes itself as a search index or an index, you choose a Gopher menu option that's named "Search Gopherspace Using Veronica" or something like that. Usually, you see a menu option that references Veronica on the main menu for a Gopher server. I'll show you how all this works with the Internet Explorer, but remember that this may work a little differently, depending on how you connect to the Internet and on your Gopher client.

1 Connect to the Internet in the usual way.

2 Start the Gopher client. (Depending on how you connect to the Internet, you may actually start the Gopher client first.)

3 Choose the Gopher menu option that references Veronica. You may
get another menu of options that let you choose the specific Gopher server that will perform the Veronica search or the type of
Veronica search: server names, directory names, and so on. If you
do, choose one of these options.

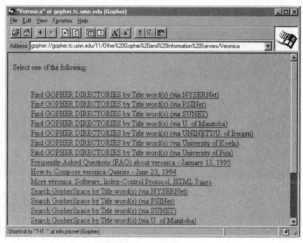

4 When prompted by the Gopher client, enter the keyword or the
keywords you want to use to search "Gopherspace."

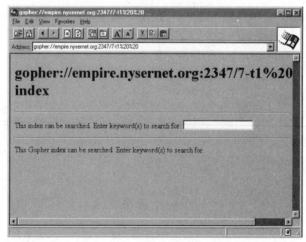

5 Initiate the search. In the case in which the Internet Explorer is the
Gopher client, you press Enter.

continues

Gopher (continued)

Once Gopher finishes its search, it displays a list of Gopher servers, directories, or menu options that match your keyword. You can then move to a server, directory, or menu option by selecting it.

Veronica is smart

I haven't described Veronica's search capabilities in much detail here. But you should know that Veronica lets you get quite sophisticated about the way you specify search criteria. You can use Boolean logic, for example. If you're interested in these kinds of advanced search techniques, keep your eyes open for a **FAQ** about Veronica. It will probably appear as another menu option near the menu option that lets you search "Gopherspace" using Veronica.

Finding Resources with Jughead

Jughead is another search tool. Jughead works sort of like Veronica and sort of like a searchable index. In effect, what Jughead searches is a searchable index of a group of Gopher servers. You usually won't see the name "Jughead" on a menu. Instead, you'll see a menu option named something like "Search Gopher Titles at the University of Minnesota."

Gulf War One of the interesting features of the Internet is that the information that gets passed around is broken into little chunks called **packets**. It's these little packets that get passed from the sending **network** to the receiving network. Different packets may actually travel different routes on the network and arrive at the receiving network in a different order. But because the Internet is set up to deal with packets sent by routes, nothing gets jumbled or lost. If a packet does get lost somewhere in route, no trouble—the system is smart enough to notice the missing packet and have it sent again. The **TCP/IP** protocol creates, tracks, and reassembles the packets.

Okay. I know this entry says "Gulf War." And you're wondering what any of this has to do with Iraq, Sadaam Hussein, Kuwait, or George Bush. But there's a connection. TCP/IP protocol exists because roughly 25 years ago the United States government needed to create a network that wouldn't get knocked out in, say, a thermonuclear exchange with the former Soviet Union. For example, if a big Internet host in, say, Chicago, got wiped out, the network needed to automatically recover and then start routing stuff through St. Louis, or Minneapolis, or wherever. The U.S., fortunately, never got a chance to test the network in a real-life setting. But, unfortunately, the Iraqis did during the Gulf War. The verdict? The rumor mill says that despite the best efforts of Norman Schwarzkopf and crew, the allies either never did shut down or had a terrible time shutting down the computer network that the Iraqis relied on for their command and control activities. And the reason the allies had so much trouble cutting Iraqi communications was because of this TCP/IP protocol stuff.

Packet Switched Network

Home Page
A home page is the first **World Wide Web** document you view with a Web **browser** such as **Internet Explorer**. You can tell your Web browser which home page it should display when you first start it. Or you can just use whatever home page the Web browser is initially set to use.

Host Computer   A host computer is just a computer that's connected to the Internet. For example, if you connect your PC to the Internet using a **PPP** connection, your PC temporarily becomes a host computer. Of course, any of the mainframe computers or minicomputers that you connect to are also host computers. (Estimates vary, but as a rough guess, there are probably over 3 million Internet host computers worldwide.)

I'm not all that fussy a person. Really. But I will be picky and tell you that if you've connected to an **access provider** using a communications application like **HyperTerminal,** your computer isn't actually a host computer. You're connected to a host computer that's part of the Internet.

 Server

Host Names   Host names provide an easy way to identify hosts so you don't have to remember a host's **IP** number. Each host name can correspond to only one IP number. Host addresses have the format *hostname.domainname*—for example, *ftp.microsoft.com*. In this case, *ftp* is the host name and *microsoft.com* is the domain name. **DNS** (domain name service), by the way, does the mapping of host names to IP numbers.

Hot Link   A hot link is what you click in a **World Wide Web** document to move from document to document. Hot links are also called hypertext links and **anchors**.

HTML   The acronym HTML stands for hypertext markup language. HTML is what you use to create **World Wide Web** documents. In fact, for this reason, the HTML acronym is often used as the last part of a World Wide Web document name—to identify what it is. (On PCs, World Wide Web documents use the **file extension** HTM for the same basic reason.) Do you need to know this? No, not really. The only time you'd even need to worry about or work with HTML is if you were creating your own World Wide Web documents.

HTTP   This acronym stands for Hypertext Transfer Protocol. HTTP is the **protocol** that makes the **World Wide Web** possible. You may actually want to remember this acronym, because the **uniform resource locator** (URL) for every World Wide Web site starts with it. For example, the Microsoft Corporation's World Wide Web site looks like this:

```
http://www.microsoft.com
```

HyperTerminal   HyperTerminal is Windows 95's powerful new communications application. With it and a **modem**, you can connect your computer to another computer, to an electronic mail service, and to many electronic bulletin board systems, or **BBSs**. If you connect to the Internet using an **access provider** and you're not making a **PPP** or **SLIP** connection, for example, you probably use HyperTerminal.

continues

HyperTerminal *(continued)*

Describing a HyperTerminal Connection

To start HyperTerminal and use it to connect to another computer, you first need to describe the connection. To do this, follow these steps:

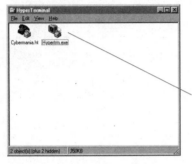

1 Click the Start button. Next, choose Programs, Accessories, and then HyperTerminal Connections.

2 Start HyperTerminal by double-clicking the Hypertrm icon. HyperTerminal starts and asks you for the name of the connection.

3 Name the HyperTerminal connection by typing the name in this text box.

4 If you want, you can also pick an icon from this box.

5 Click OK. HyperTerminal asks you for the telephone number—and for some other information as well.

6 Type the telephone number here. (If necessary, you can also specify the country code and area code with the other boxes.)

7 Verify that the Connect Using drop-down list box specifies your modem.

8 Click OK. HyperTerminal asks for just a bit more information so that it can dial the telephone number.

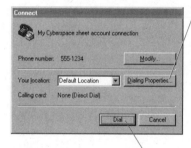

9 Click Dialing Properties if this is a long-distance telephone call, if you need to fiddle with things like calling cards, or if you need to precede the telephone number with a number to get an outside line. Use the dialog box that HyperTerminal displays to specify these extra bits of telephone trivia.

10 To dial the telephone number so that you can connect to the other computer, click Dial.

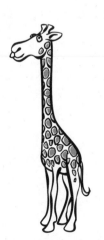

continues

HyperTerminal *(continued)*

Saving the HyperTerminal Connection Description

You'll want to save the HyperTerminal connection description so you can make the connection again. To do so, follow these steps:

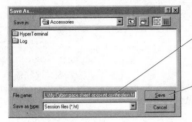

1 Choose the File Save As command.

2 Enter a **file name** for the HyperTerminal description.

3 Click Save.

Connecting to Another Computer

Once you've described a connection, connecting subsequent times is easy. First, you click the Start button. Then choose Programs, Accessories, and HyperTerminal Connections.

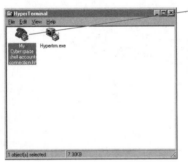

To connect, double-click a connection description. HyperTerminal displays the Connect dialog box (which I just showed). You click Dial to start HyperTerminal and connect to the other computer.

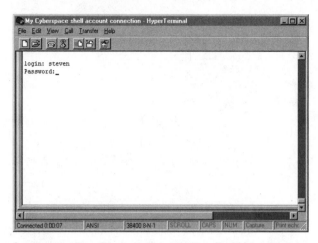

Once you start HyperTerminal, you see the HyperTerminal application window on your screen. To connect to the other computer, you probably need to do whatever it wants—provide a **username** and **password** for example— but you might need to supply other information. It depends.

Working Once You're Connected

Once you connect to another computer, your computer is essentially just a "dumb terminal." In other words, you use your keyboard and your monitor, but it's really the other computer and its software that you're using. If you connect to a **BBS** (bulletin board system), for example, you'll probably see menus of commands that you can use to do different stuff.

Downloading Files

To move **files** to your computer from the computer to which you're connected, you first tell the other computer that you want it to send a file or a batch of files. (If you've connected to an access provider that uses the **UNIX** operating system, you can probably type the command *sz* followed by the file name. For example, to download a file named *secrets.doc,* you type *sz secrets.doc.*)

If you're using the **Zmodem** protocol, that's all you have to do. HyperTerminal displays a dialog box that reports on the file being sent from the other computer.

continues

HyperTerminal *(continued)*

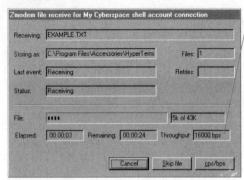

You can tell how fast the transfer is going by looking at the Throughput box.

If you're using some other protocol, you tell the other computer that you want it to send a file. (Again, you do this by issuing a command such as *sx*, which means "send file using Xmodem," followed by the file name.) Then—usually after you've been prompted by the other computer—you choose the Transfer Receive File command.

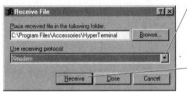

Activate this drop-down list box to specify the protocol as Xmodem, Kermit, or whatever.

Click Receive after you pick a protocol.

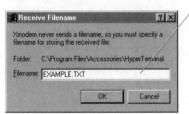

Name the file you will receive. Then click OK.

Zmodem is best

If you have a choice of file transfer protocols, choose Zmodem. Zmodem is easier to use because you don't have to mess with the protocol or name the files you're receiving. And Zmodem lets you receive more than one file at a time by using **wildcard characters.** Best of all, Zmodem is much, much faster than other protocols. For example, one afternoon when I should have been working but was instead surfing the Internet, my throughput using Zmodem was around 16,000 **bits per second,** but my throughput using Xmodem was around 4,000 bits per second.

Uploading Files

To send a file from your computer to the other computer, first do whatever gets the other computer ready. If your access provider uses UNIX, for example, you can type the command for receiving files using the Zmodem protocol, *rz*. Then choose the Transfer Send File command. HyperTerminal displays a dialog box that asks for the file name, the location, and which file transfer protocol you want to use.

Identify the file and its location.

Choose a file transfer protocol.

This dialog box describes the file transfer progress.

The Throughput box shows you how fast files are transferring.

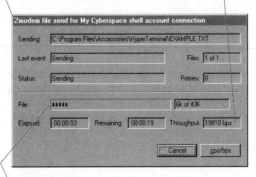

This progress bar shows you how far along the file transfer is.

continues

73

HyperTerminal *(continued)*

Describing the Communications Protocol

With HyperTerminal, you usually don't have to worry about the communications protocol. HyperTerminal examines your modem, figures out what it can do, and then works with the other computer to make your communications as fast and smooth as possible.

This means you shouldn't ever have to worry about things like data bits, stop bits, parity, and flow control. Sure, these details are important to HyperTerminal. They describe how the data is transmitted between your computer and the one it's connected to. But HyperTerminal usually takes care of the details.

Disconnecting from Another Computer

To disconnect from another computer, first complete any disconnection instructions provided by the electronic mail service or bulletin board system. Then choose the Call Disconnect command.

.·. **Troubleshooting: HyperTerminal; Quick Reference: HyperTerminal Command Guide *and* HyperTerminal Toolbar Guide**

Internet Address When common folk like you and me use the term "Internet address," we probably mean the **username** and **domain name** that are used to e-mail someone. If you want to e-mail the President of the United States, for example, you can use this address:

`president@whitehouse.gov`

The *president* part of the address is the person's name (or, in this case, the person's title). The *whitehouse.gov* part of the address is the domain name. This makes sense, right? (By the way, if you want to talk the talk, you describe this address as "president at Whitehouse dot gov." The @ symbol is called "at.")

If you want to get technical, however, Internet addresses and **IP addresses** are two different things. IP addresses are the numbers that identify a specific host and domain. We could talk about IP addresses, but let's not. Unless you're setting up a **PPP** or **SLIP** connection, you'll never encounter them. And even then, you'll only have to noodle around with them once.

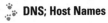 **DNS; Host Names**

Internet Explorer Plus! for Windows 95 comes with its own Web **browser**, Internet Explorer. You use the Internet Explorer to browse the **World Wide Web,** to view **newsgroups,** to use **Gopher,** and to **FTP.**

Starting the Internet Explorer

To start the Internet Explorer, you just double-click on the Internet icon, which appears on your **desktop**. When you do, the Internet Explorer displays your **home page.**

To connect to the Internet, enter a **uniform resource locator** into the Address box. Or choose the File Open command and enter or select a uniform resource locator from the Address box. Then click OK. Internet Explorer displays a dialog box that provides your **username, password,** and **access provider** telephone number. Verify that these are correct and click OK.

By the way, if you're already connected to the Internet—say because you're already using another Internet client—you won't need to make the connection again. So you won't see the dialog box that provides your username, password, and access provider's telephone number.

continues

Internet Explorer *(continued)*

Viewing the World Wide Web

Once you've loaded your home page, you can view it by scrolling up and down. To move to another World Wide Web document, you click a **hot link** in the currently displayed document. (The mouse pointer changes to a pointing finger whenever it rests over a hot link.) You can also move to another World Wide Web document by entering a new uniform resource locator in the Address box. To move back and forth between World Wide Web pages you've already viewed, you click the Back and Forward tools.

Whenever this logo is flashing, Internet Explorer is busy retrieving a World Wide Web document.

This is a World Wide Web document.

Viewing Graphics with the Internet Explorer

Internet Explorer comes with **GIF** and **JPEG** viewers built right into it. If you're viewing a World Wide Web document that shows a graphic image, it's usually a GIF file. Often you can click the GIF image or its icon to move to a full-screen JPEG image. (You'll be able to tell when this is the case. The status bar of the Internet Explorer will say that the graphic image is a shortcut to some other file.)

You can save full-screen GIF and JPEG images displayed in the Internet Explorer window by choosing the File Save As command. When Internet Explorer displays the Save As dialog box, use the Save In and File Name boxes to specify where you want the file saved and what you want it named.

To view a GIF or JPEG file you've previously saved to disk using the Internet Explorer, choose the File Open command. When Internet Explorer displays the Open Internet address dialog box, click the Open File command button. When Internet Explorer displays the Open File dialog box, first activate the Files of Type box and select either the GIF or JPEG file type, and then use the Look In and File Name box to locate and identify the file.

Why the image changes

If you look closely, you'll notice that some graphic images in World Wide Web documents look fuzzy at first but then become more and more focused. What you're seeing, just in case you care, is something called *progressive rendering*. As the World Wide Web server sends its image to your PC, your PC keeps drawing a better and clearer image the more information it gets.

Viewing Newsgroups

Although you can view newsgroups with some Web browsers, you can't view them using **Internet Explorer.** If you've got a PPP connection, you can use a shareware **newsgroup** reader client. (Windows 95, unfortunately, expects you to view newsgroups from The **Microsoft Network.**)

Telnetting

While you can **Telnet** with some Web browsers, you can't with Internet Explorer. Windows 95, however, comes with a Telnet client. Refer to the Telnet entry for more information.

Using Gopher

You can explore "Gopherspace" using Internet Explorer. To do this, just enter a Gopher server **uniform resource locator** in the Address box. I describe how you do this in more detail in the **Gopher** entry.

continues

Internet Explorer *(continued)*

Using FTP

To **FTP** with the Internet Explorer, just enter an FTP server's uniform resource locator such as *ftp://ftp.microsoft.com* in the Address box. The Internet Explorer will display a list of directories and **files** at the FTP site.

This is the way an FTP site looks when viewed with the Internet Explorer.

To view the files in a directory, click the directory. To view the contents of a file, click the file. (You can usually identify file types by looking at their **file extensions.)** To save a file, choose the File Save As command and fill in the dialog box that Internet Explorer displays.

Printing World Wide Web documents

The Internet Explorer provides a File Print command. You can use it to print the text portions of the Web document shown in the Internet Explorer window. Well, actually that's not quite right. What you really do is print the **HTML** document that produces the World Wide Web page you see on your screen. This HTML document includes all the text as well as the formatting instructions used to display the document.

To use the File Print command, display the Web page you want to print, choose the command, and then click OK when Internet Explorer displays the Print dialog box.

Saving World Wide Web documents

The Internet Explorer also provides a File Save command. You can use it to save the HTML document that produces the World Wide Web page you see on your screen. To use this command, just choose it. When Internet Explorer displays the Save dialog box, use it to name the document.

Disconnecting from the Internet

When you're done using any Internet client—including Internet Explorer—you need to disconnect your PC from the Internet. To do this, click the Connection button that appears on the Taskbar. When the Connected dialog box appears, click Disconnect.

The name of this dialog box shows your access provider's name. So your dialog box will probably be different.

⁂ **Quick Reference: Internet Explorer Commands *and* Internet Explorer Toolbar Guide**

Internet Service Provider ⁂ Access Provider

Internet Setup Wizard
When you install Microsoft Plus! for Windows 95, if you indicate that you want the Internet Jumpstart Kit installed, the setup program runs the Internet Setup Wizard. This wizard collects the information that Plus! needs to connect to the Internet. I'm not going to describe here how you use the Internet Setup Wizard. It's simply a matter of clicking buttons and filling in a few dialog boxes. Just follow the onscreen instructions and you'll be fine.

By the way, the wizard will prompt you for several pieces of information, including your **access provider's** name and telephone number, your **username,** and your **password.** You need to get all of this information from your access provider before you run the wizard. (Just call your provider and ask for whatever information you need to set up your account under Windows 95.)

Internet Society The Internet Society is an international organization that coordinates the Internet and its internetworking technologies and applications. You can find more information about the Internet Society at the **World Wide Web** site *http://www.isoc.org.*

InterNIC This sounds like some espionage organization, doesn't it? Like some super-secret agency you'd read about in a John LeCarre spy novel, maybe. Or, at the very least, like some regular band of villains on "Get Smart."

But actually, InterNIC refers to the Internet Network Information Center. The InterNIC stores information about the Internet. The InterNIC, for example, has information about all the various Internet standards that define and describe the **network** itself. The InterNIC also has information about a bunch of FTP sites. Its **uniform resource locator** is *ftp.internic.net.*

IP IP is an acronym for internet protocol. It is the Network Layer in the **TCP/IP** protocol. It ensures that **packets** get delivered to the correct destinations. IP is also the protocol after which the Internet was named.

IP Address The IP address is the numeric address of a **host computer.** As a practical matter, you never need to worry about IP addresses unless you're involved in setting up a **PPP** or **SLIP** connection. You do need to worry about the **Internet addresses** of everyone you want to send **e-mail** to, however.

 DNS

JPEG   JPEG is a graphics file format. (The name is actually an acronym for Joint Photographic Experts Group.) Basically, the JPEG file format was created because people felt that other graphics file formats, including the ever-popular **GIF** format, were too big. Some people think that JPEG is inferior to GIF. But high-quality JPEGs, in my humble opinion, look just as good as high-quality GIFs. And they're always significantly smaller. You can identify JPEG files because they have the letters . JPG as their **file extensions.**

To view a JPEG file, you'll either need a **browser** with an internal JPEG **viewer**—like **Internet Explorer**—or an external viewer. Any viewer deserving of the name, however, will let you view JPEG files.

Kilobyte   I know you didn't buy this book to learn about the guts of your computer. But since I've used the term kilobyte in a couple of places, I thought I should at least define it. Okay? Good. A byte is an eight-digit string of 1s and 0s that your computer uses to represent a character. (These 1s and 0s are called **bits.**) This, for example, is a byte:

01010100

A kilobyte is roughly 1,000 of these bytes. (Or, to be just excruciatingly precise, a kilobyte is exactly 1,024 of these bytes.)

 Megabyte

LAN   LAN is an acronym for local area **network.** A LAN, for example, might connect all the computers in an office or in a building. You hear this term a lot in discussions about the Internet. I don't know why. Whether an Internet **host** is on a LAN, a **MAN,** or a **WAN** makes little difference.

LISTSERV LISTSERV is one of the more popular **mailing list** manager programs. (The other two mailing list programs you often see are LISTPROC and Majordomo.) So what does a mailing list manager program do? Simple. It adds users to and removes users from a mailing list. You can tell whether LISTSERV is the program used to maintain a particular mailing list because the **e-mail** address to which you send your subscription and termination requests will have LISTSERV in its name.

Log On Logging on is what you do to connect to an Internet **host**. Specifically, logging on means to give your **username** and a **password** when you start using a computer.

Lurk As far as your neighbor's rhododendron beds go, lurking is a bad thing. Especially if done at night. You don't want to lurk. You may get arrested.

In a **newsgroup** or **mailing list,** however, lurking is good. It means to quietly observe. It means to read the posted messages and get a feel for what goes on and what doesn't before posting a message yourself. By lurking, you won't post a stupid message and get **flamed.**

Mailing List On the Internet, a mailing list is just a list of people who want to receive information via e-mail about a particular topic. BMW motorcycles. A particular television show. Some quirky author. If you want to receive information about a particular topic covered by a mailing list, you ask the mailing list administrator to have your name added to the mailing list. If you have something relevant to say about a topic, you can **e-mail** a message to the mailing list. And everybody on the mailing list gets your message.

Finding the Mailing List You Want

Many, many mailing lists exist. So it can be a little difficult to find one that matches your interest. The phrase "needle in a haystack" comes to mind. You can, however, get a list of mailing lists from this **anonymous FTP** site: *ftp://rtfm.mit.edu/pub/usenet/news.answers/mail/mailing-lists*. What you want to do is get the **file** named part01 and at least a few of the other "part" files listed at this site. To start, for example, get part02 and part03, print these text files (you can use Windows 95's **WordPad** utility to do this), and read through the stuff. Take it from there.

Subscribing to a Mailing List Administered by a Person

To get your name added to a mailing list, you need to know the e-mail address of the mailing list administrator. Once you know this, you just e-mail a message to the address. The subject of the message should be "subscribe to mailing list" and the message text should say, "subscribe" followed by your first and last name. (By the way, if you're in a friendly mood, you might include some other chitchat, too. That's okay. Remember that you're communicating with a real person.)

Here's an example. If I wanted to subscribe to the mailing list *bbshop-request@cray.com*, a barbershop quartet mailing list, I would send the following e-mail message:

```
To:        bbshop-request@cray.com
Subject:   subscribe to mailing list
Message:   subscribe Steve Nelson
```

A tip for new mailing list subscribers

You probably don't want to subscribe to a bunch of mailing lists right off the bat. Instead, subscribe to one or two. Or maybe three at the most. Otherwise, you'll find yourself overwhelmed with e-mail. And you don't want that to happen.

Mailing List (continued)

Unsubscribing from a Mailing List Administered by a Person

To have your name removed from a mailing list, you just e-mail a message to the list administrator's address. The subject should be "unsubscribe to mailing list" and the text should say, "unsubscribe" followed by your first and last name. For example, if I wanted to unsubscribe to the mailing list *bbshop-request@cray.com*, I would send the following e-mail message:

```
To:        bbshop-request@cray.com
Subject:   unsubscribe to mailing list
Message:   unsubscribe Steve Nelson
```

A mailing list faux pas

When you send a subscription request, be sure you send your e-mail message to the mailing list administrator. You don't want to send the subscription request to the mailing list. Oh no. If you do, you'll be mailing your request to everyone on the list. The mailing list administrator's e-mail address is usually named *list-request*, where *list* is the name of the mailing list. Does that make sense? So if the mailing list name is *bbshop*, the mailing list administrator's address is probably *bbshop-request*.

Subscribing to a Mailing List Administered by a Program

One thing that is sort of confusing about this whole mailing list business is that some mailing lists aren't administered by a person. Some of them are administered by programs named things like majordomo, **LISTSERV,** or LISTPROC. If the **username** that you e-mail your subscription request to is, for example, majordomo, LISTSERV, or LISTPROC, you are actually sending your subscription request to the program that administers the mailing list. To learn the correct name of the program, site, and domain, you probably have to get the skinny from someone who's already subscribed. Or you have to get more detailed information about the mailing list. (For example, you could get the mailing list subscription information from the **anonymous** FTP site I described earlier.)

Once you get this information, you subscribe by sending the administrator an e-mail message that includes the command *subscribe*, the name of the mailing list, and your name. (But you don't need to include anything on the Subject line.) For example, to subscribe to the mailing list 2020world, I would send my subscription request to *majordomo@seatimes.com*. My e-mail message would look like this:

```
To:         majordomo@seatimes.com
Subject:
Message:    subscribe 2020world Steve Nelson
```

Unsubscribing to a Mailing List Administered by a Program

To have your name removed from a mailing list administered by a program like majordomo, LISTSERV, or LISTPROC, you just e-mail a message to the administrator and include the appropriate unsubscribe command. (As with your subscription request, you can just leave the Subject line blank.) Which command you use to unsubscribe, however, depends on the mailing list administrator program. If the program is LISTPROC or majordomo, you use the command *unsubscribe* and the name of the mailing list. For example, if I wanted to unsubscribe to the 2020world mailing list, I would send the following e-mail message:

```
To:         majordomo@seatimes.com
Subject:
Message:    unsubscribe 2020world
```

If the program is LISTSERV, you use the command *signoff* and the name of the mailing list. For example, if I wanted to unsubscribe from a mailing list named beerlovers maintained by the LISTSERV program at *ryderwood.edu*, I would send the following e-mail message:

```
To:         listserv@ryderwood.edu
Subject:
Message:    signoff beerlovers
```

For more help request help

The mailing list administrator programs—LISTPROC, LISTSERV, and major-domo—offer more commands than I've described here. You can usually get a list of the commands (with descriptions) that a mailing list administrator program uses by sending the one-word message help to the mailing list administrator.

 FTP

MAN

MAN has two meanings. The MAN acronym—all upper-case letters—stands for metropolitan area **network**. Not knowing this term wouldn't make you less of a cybernaut, but you do sometimes hear people use it. Especially technical types who want to distinguish this type of network from a **LAN**, or local area network, and a **WAN**, or wide area network.

The **UNIX** operating system provides a *man* command—all lowercase letters. The *man* command opens up a "manual" of online help. This nugget of knowledge is a good one to remember.

Megabyte

As you may already know, a byte is an eight-digit string of 1s and 0s that your computer uses to represent a character. This, for example, is the byte that represents the character A:

01010100.

A **kilobyte** is roughly 1,000 of these bytes. (Or, to be precise, a kilobyte is 1,024 of these bytes.)

A megabyte is roughly 1,000,000 of these bytes. (Again, if you want to be precise, a megabyte is exactly 1,048,576 bytes. Oh my.)

Another way to look at a megabyte is in terms of how long it would take you to **download** or **upload** a megabyte of stuff. With a **modem** and a communications protocol such as **Zmodem** that passes the data through at a rate of 14,400 bps, or 14.4Kbps, it would take around 10 minutes to download or upload a megabyte of stuff.

MPEG MPEG is a graphics file format for video, or movies. (The acronym stands for Moving Photographic Experts Group.) Like **JPEG**, MPEG was developed to provide a very efficient and compressed format for storing high-quality video. To view an MPEG file, you need an MPEG viewer.

Microsoft Exchange You use Microsoft Exchange to send and read **e-mail** messages if you've made a **PPP** connection to the Internet or you are using the **Microsoft Network** to connect to the Internet. To use Microsoft Exchange you first need to make the connection. Then you start Exchange, such as by clicking the Start button and then choosing Programs and Microsoft Exchange.

continues

Microsoft Exchange *(continued)*

Sending an E-Mail Message

To send an e-mail message to someone, follow these steps:

1 Choose the Compose New Message command. Exchange displays the New Message window and starts your e-mail editor. (In my case, the e-mail editor is Microsoft Word. If you've set up Exchange to use a different e-mail editor, your new message window will look slightly different.)

2 Enter the recipient's e-mail address in the To box. If you want to send the message to more than one person, separate the e-mail names with semicolons.

3 Optionally, enter the e-mail name or names of anyone you want to receive a copy of the e-mail message in the Cc box.

4 Enter a brief description of your message in the Subject box.

5 Use the main message text area beneath the To, Cc, and Subject boxes to write your message.

6 To send your message when you're done writing it, choose the File Send command.

Formatting e-mail messages

If your e-mail allows, you'll be able to format your e-mail message in a number of different ways. Because I use Microsoft Word for Windows 95 as my e-mail editor, for example, I can do a bunch of fancy formatting.

Reading E-Mail Messages You Receive

To read an e-mail message somebody sends you, start Microsoft Exchange and click the Inbox icon in the **folder pane** portion of the Exchange window. This tells Exchange to list any messages people have sent you in the message page portion of the Exchange window.

Click this icon to open the Inbox.

Exchange lists any messages you've received in the message pane. To read one of your messages, click it. Exchange displays the Read message window with the selected message.

Once you're done with your message, you can delete it by clicking the Delete tool.

You can forward the message to someone else by choosing the Compose Forward command or the Forward tool and then, when prompted, by specifying the e-mail address of the person you want to forward the message to.

Replying to E-Mail Messages

You can reply to a message by choosing the Compose Reply To Sender command or the Reply To Sender tool or by choosing the Compose Reply To All tool. When you reply to a message, Exchange opens the Reply To A Message window, fills in the To box and Subject boxes for you, and copies the original message to the message text area. You can then add your reply to the message text area.

continues

Microsoft Exchange *(continued)*

Sending Files with E-Mail Messages

You should be able to send files with e-mail messages. But the mechanics of doing this depends on your e-mail editor. If you're using Word as your e-mail editor, for example, you insert a file in the e-mail message using Word's Insert File command.

Exchange handles files inserted in e-mail messages either by using **MIME** (which is the default) or by uuencoding the file (thereby converting the file into text). The only trick to sending and receiving files is that the sender and recipient need to handle the file in the same way. If the sender uses MIME, the recipient needs to use MIME. If the sender uses uuencode, the recipient needs to use a uudecoder.

To change the way Exchange handles files, follow these steps:

1 Choose the Tools Services command. Exchange displays the Services dialog box.

2 Select the Internet Mail entry in the only list box displayed on the Services dialog box.

3 Click Properties. Exchange displays the Internet Mail dialog box.

4 Click Message Format. Exchange displays the Message Format dialog box.

5 Click either the MIME or Uuencode button, as appropriate.

 Encoded Files

Microsoft Network Microsoft Network, or more precisely, The Microsoft Network, is the name of Microsoft's **online service.** I mention this here because The Microsoft Network provides an easy way to connect to the Internet. (In fact, if you run the **Internet Setup Wizard** that comes with Plus! for Windows 95, it assumes you want to connect to the Internet by using The Microsoft Network.) With the version of Microsoft Network that's available as I'm writing this, you can send and receive e-mail, participate in **mailing lists,** and read and post messages to **newsgroups.** In the near future, so the rumor is, you'll even be able to browse the **World Wide Web.** (And that should also mean you'll be able to **FTP.**)

Using E-Mail with The Microsoft Network

To send and read an e-mail message with The Microsoft Network, you use **Microsoft Exchange.** To use Exchange with The Microsoft Network, start Microsoft Network and then click on the E-Mail button on the Microsoft Network home page.

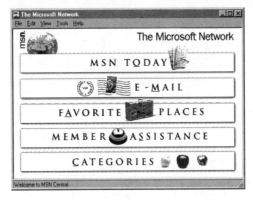

Browsing Newsgroups with The Microsoft Network

To browse a newsgroup with The Microsoft Network, follow these steps:

1 Start The Microsoft Network. The Microsoft Network displays the Home Base window.

2 Click the Categories button on the Home Base window. The Microsoft Network displays a list of information **folders** in the **folders pane.**

continues

Microsoft Network *(continued)*

3 Double-click the Internet Center icon. The Microsoft Network displays the Internet Center window.

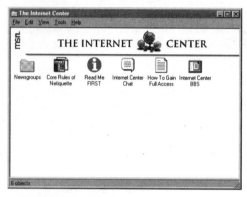

4 Double-click the Newsgroups icon. The Microsoft Network displays the Newsgroups window.

5 Double-click the Usenet Newsgroups icon. Microsoft Network displays a list of newsgroup categories.

6 Double-click one of the Newsgroups categories. Microsoft Network displays a list of specific newsgroups within the selected category.

7 Double-click one of the newsgroups in the selected category. Microsoft Network displays the articles, or posted messages, for the selected newsgroup.

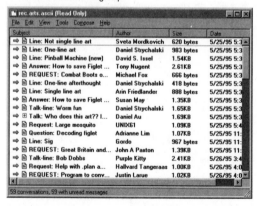

8 Double-click the **article,** or posted message, you want to read. You'll probably need to scroll through the list of articles to find the one you want.

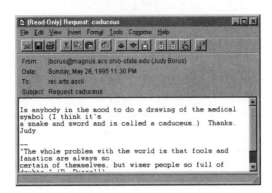

🐾 **Internet Explorer**

MIME

MIME stands for "multipurpose Internet mail extensions." MIME is a protocol that lets you attach binary files—like **JPEG** files, **GIF** files, **MPEG** files, and so on—to **e-mail** messages. As long as the people you send messages to also have e-mail readers that support the MIME protocol, they can extract and use the files you send them. For example, you could use MIME to stick a Microsoft Word for Windows document in an e-mail message. If the recipient's e-mail reader supports MIME, the recipient can extract the Word document from the e-mail message. If the recipient has a copy of Word for Windows, he or she can open and work with the document in Word.

🐾 **PINE**

Modem A modem—the word means *modulator/demodulator*—is a hardware device for sending **files** and messages over the telephone lines. To send a file or message, the modem converts computer data into sounds and sends the sounds over the telephone line to another modem and computer at the other end of the telephone line. To receive a file or message, the modem hears the sounds coming over the telephone line and converts the sounds back into digital code that a computer can read.

How fast a modem can send or receive data is measured in **bits per second,** or bps. Modems with higher bps rates can send and receive data faster. When you are shopping for a modem, buy a 14,400bps or 28,800bps model. They cost more, but you'll save money in the long run because you won't spend as much time using **online services,** which charge by the hour. Fast modems can download information quicker.

Baud; Downloading Files

Moderator A moderator is someone who decides which **articles** are posted to a **newsgroup** or which e-mail messages are sent to the people on a **mailing list.** A newsgroup or mailing list that has one of these characters is called, cleverly enough, a moderated newsgroup or moderated mailing list.

For the readers or users of a newsgroup or mailing list, moderators are wonderful. They make sure that people stay on track. And they weed out the silly articles and messages that waste people's time and disk space. In fact, if I was to offer a single suggestion for making the best use of your time with things like newsgroups and mailing lists, I'd suggest that you stick to those with moderators.

Unfortunately, if you're trying to post stuff to a newsgroup or send e-mail messages to a mailing list, moderators can be really frustrating. They might seem like censors. Sometimes they filter out the most cogent and poignant ideas. And, darn it, they always take a while to review the articles and messages you want to post. Almost as if they have a life outside their probably-unpaid duty as moderator. Perhaps they have jobs or families, for instance.

 Netiquette

Mosaic

NCSA Mosaic is a Web **browser** you use to look at **World Wide Web** documents. In fact, Microsoft's Internet Explorer is based on technology licensed from the National Center of Supercomputing Applications (NCSA), the creators of Mosaic. You can actually get a free copy of this program at *ftp.ncsa.uiuc.edu.* I don't cover the details of using NCSA Mosaic here. But one Web browser works pretty much like another. So if you're using Mosaic and reading this book, take a peek at the entry on **Internet Explorer.**

Multitasking

Multitasking refers to the running of more than one application at the same time. You may not think you care about this, but actually you do. Because Windows 95 lets you smoothly multitask, you can be working away with your word processor, for example, at the same time as **HyperTerminal** or **Internet Explorer** is slaving away to **download** a huge **file.** Windows 95 automatically multitasks Windows 95-based applications. Whenever you or Windows 95 opens more than one Windows-based application, you're multitasking. Pretty cool, huh?

To switch between the applications you're running, just click application buttons on the Taskbar.

Switching Tasks

Name Server ❖ Domain Name Service

Netiquette Netiquette is the special word that's been coined to describe Internet etiquette. You know what I'm describing here, right? Good manners. Proper conduct. That sort of thing. Fortunately, Internet etiquette—netiquette— isn't as complicated as the etiquette rules for going to dinner at, say, Buckingham Palace or the White House. There, so I've read, you have to know about all sorts of stuff. Like which of the four forks to use. (Actually, I happen to know the answer to this one: Just start with the fork farthest to the left and work your way inward, or toward the plate, as the courses arrive on the table. But back to the Internet...)

On the Internet, you just have to be a nice guy or gal. If an organization lets you anonymously **Telnet** or **FTP** from their host, follow any rules they suggest for usage. (Like hours the host can be accessed.) Don't **flame** people. Don't post **articles** that waste people's time to **newsgroups**. (Don't, for example, post a "Me, too!" message.) Don't **spam**. And, for gosh sakes, make sure you post articles to the correct newsgroup.

Since many readers will connect to the Internet using The **Microsoft Network,** let me also share a quick story about what happened when **America Online,** another **online service,** provided **gateways** to the Internet for its subscribers. As a group, America Online subscribers developed a terrible reputation because so many of them completely ignored netiquette. In some newsgroups, the regulars got so tired of these **newbies** that they openly talked about methods for blocking access to the AOLers. Suffice it to say, things got ugly. So let's not let the same thing happen with The Microsoft Network. Okay?

❖ **RTFM; Shouting**

Network A network is just a bunch of computers that are connected together. Windows 95, for example, lets you create what are called peer-to-peer networks as long as you've got **Ethernet** cards installed in the computers and the right kind of cabling to connect the Ethernet cards. But I'm getting off the track. The reason I mention this is because the Internet is really a network of networks. But one thing I probably should mention is that while all of the individual networks, or subnets, that make up the Internet are **TCP/IP** networks, the individual hosts use a bunch of different operating systems. Some of these hosts use Windows 95 for their operating system. But other hosts use **UNIX**, Windows NT, and even DEC and IBM mainframe and minicomputer operating systems.

Newbie A newbie is someone who's new to the neighborhood—the Internet neighborhood, that is. Everybody on the Internet was a newbie once, of course. But many experienced veterans of the Internet forget this. So newbies often get picked on. Probably the best way to avoid this abuse is to be sensitive to the informal rules and protocols of the Internet, which will minimize mistakes on your part.

I may as well mention here, too, that if you're an **America Online** user and that's how you've connected to the Internet, the America Online **domain name** that gets tagged to the end of your postings, *aol.com*, will instantly identify you as a possible newbie. Newbies can become rather a nuisance on the Internet because many of them don't **lurk,** they ignore the **FAQs,** and they refuse to **RTFM.**

Netiquette

Newsgroup A newsgroup is basically an electronic corkboard where people post and read messages related to a particular topic or interest. For free. And with more than 10,000 active newsgroups, there's a newsgroup on just about every topic imaginable. In fact, I think it's fair to say that newsgroups are probably one of the three most popular **resources** available on the Internet. (**E-mail** and the **World Wide Web** are the other two.)

To write messages for and read messages on a newsgroup, you need a newsgroup reader. If you're connecting to the Internet with a **shell account,** for example, you need to use something like **TIN.** (I wrote a special entry for using TIN, so you can refer there if you want to use it.) If you're connecting to the Internet with a **PPP** or **SLIP** connection, you need to use a newsgroup **viewer** or Web **browser** that reads and writes to newsgroups. The **Internet Explorer**—unlike some Web browsers—doesn't let you view newsgroups. But almost certainly your access provider will provide another newsgroup reader you can use if you connect using a PPP connection. If you're connecting to the Internet using an **online service** like The **Microsoft Network,** the online service will include commands that let you browse and post messages to newsgroups.

Some of you are curious, so I'll tell you right now

Okay, let's face up to a fact. One of the most notorious elements of the Internet is all the material on sexual themes. Presumably, you already know this, right? You've read the articles about people being arrested. You've read the articles about pornography being stored on university and government computer **networks**. I'm not telling you stuff you don't already know, right? You didn't just fall off the turnip truck. Since you already know all of this stuff, you should know that for the most part the newsgroups are where all of this stuff is stored. See the **Sex** entry if you want more information.

Free Speech; PGP; Troubleshooting: Newsgroups

NNTP This acronym stands for Network News Transfer Protocol. You sometimes see NNTP used as an adjective to describe a news **server**. Other than this, though, you won't really have to use this acronym. You don't, for example, use the acronym NNTP in **uniform resource locators.**

 Newsgroup; Protocol

NSFNET The NSFNET was a high-speed **network** of supercomputers connected by things like fiber-optic cables and microwave and satellite links. Until April of 1995, this network—it was funded by the National Science Foundation (NSF)—was the backbone of the Internet in the United States. (Other countries have their own equivalent backbones.) What was the old NSFNET backbone is now controlled by SprintNet.

ARPA

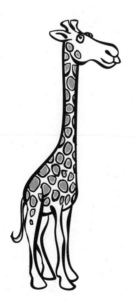

Online Services   The term online services refers to a big computer **network** with a bunch of good **files** and programs. Whoever owns this big computer network makes money by selling people like you and me access to the files stored on the network and by renting us programs on the network. Every online service, for example, provides **e-mail** so you can e-mail other online service users. (Most online services—and perhaps all the online services—also provide e-mail **gateways** to the Internet.) Online services also provide you with other stuff. Usually, there are good games you can play, neat files you can download, and up-to-the-minute news services that let you know what's happening all over the world. The **Microsoft Network** is an online service. So are **America Online**, CompuServe, and Prodigy.

   Downloading Files; Outernet

Outernet   A while back, someone coined the term "outernet" to point out a fact: **Online services** like **America Online**, CompuServe, Prodigy, and The **Microsoft Network** aren't really part of the Internet even though they are connected to the Internet via **gateways**. This doesn't mean you should suddenly feel embarrassed or like less of a person because you're not really on the Internet. You're just on the outernet. Because of the gateways, you can still do just about anything that someone with a real Internet account can do. In addition, you get whatever features the online service provides.

Packets

Everything—all the information—that gets passed around the Internet is passed as a packet. When you send some piece of information, for example, it is broken down into packets by the sending computer and then reassembled by the receiving computer. In fact, this packetizing and unpacketizing is what the **TCP/IP** protocol does.

Gulf War; Packet Switched Network

Packet Switched Network

For all I know, you stumbled onto this entry by mistake. But since you're already here, let me explain why I included this entry in the book. The Internet, it turns out, is a packet switched network. What this means is that when two computers communicate over the **network**, they break their data into **packets**, and then the packets get passed around the network. The unique thing about a packet switched network, at least when compared to a **circuit switched network**, is that the packets don't have to travel on their own dedicated connection. In fact, one writer has used the analogy of the post office to explain what a packet switched network is like. When you send something by **snail mail**, or regular mail, your letter or package doesn't get its own special airplane or mail truck. Instead, it gets bundled with a bunch of other people's mail. Only when the mail gets closer to its destination does it get separated into a little bundle of its own that the mail carrier drops into your mailbox.

A minor technical detail

There's another interesting aspect to a packet switched network. Your packets don't have to travel the same route between the sending and receiving hosts. One packet might go through St. Louis on its way from Seattle to Miami. Another packet might instead go through Cincinnati even though this packet is part of the very same message.

Gulf War

Password

You know what a password is, right? It's the secret word or code that you give to a computer, along with your **username**, to prove your identity. The logic of a password, of course, is that only the real user knows the real password, so access to the computer can be restricted to the person who is supposed to use it. There are, however, three rules concerning passwords. One rule is that your password shouldn't be easy to guess. (Don't use your name, for example.) The second rule is that you shouldn't forget your password. The third rule is that you should never tell anyone your password.

PGP

PGP is an **encryption** utility. It encrypts—or turns into coded messages—things like **e-mail** messages. Once a message has been encrypted using PGP, no one but the intended recipient can read it. So PGP is sort of interesting to people who use the Internet. Of more interest, however, is the story of how PGP was created and what happened to the creator.

Briefly, in the mid-1980s, a college student named Phillip Zimmerman read an article in the *Smithsonian* magazine that described encryption algorithms (calculation rules, basically) that made it nearly impossible for anyone other than the intended recipient to read messages. So what did the kid do? Shoot, he did what every good computer science student would do. Working on his own, he created a software program that implements the encryption algorithms.

Anyway, time goes by. By now it's the early 1990s and everything is cruising along smoothly—until one day when one of Zimmerman's friends posts Zimmerman's PGP utility on the Internet. The next thing you know, people around the world are downloading copies of this tool. And that was nice for them. But not for Zimmerman.

It turns out that the United States has strict export restrictions that severely limit the ability of Americans and American companies from selling or distributing encryption technology. And Zimmerman may have violated those export restrictions by making PGP available on the Internet, because the Internet is a global network. At the time I'm writing this, in fact, the U.S. Attorney's office in San Jose is investigating Zimmerman's actions. He could be imprisoned for as long as 5 years. And he could be fined as much as $1 million. Bummer.

The story of PGP is a really good one, however, because it touches on a couple of important points about the Internet. First, the Internet is not a very secure network. Although not very likely, it's technically possible for text that gets passed around to be read by people if they want to read it. (This is why, so the rumor mill says, the U.S. doesn't want encryption technology distributed abroad: The Central Intelligence Agency and National Security Agency want to electronically eavesdrop on people.)

A second thing that the PGP story shows is that it's easier than you think to break the law. Maybe Zimmerman or his friend knew that distributing the implementation of the algorithm—the same algorithm described in an internationally distributed magazine—would violate an export restriction. But I'll bet you a cup of coffee they didn't know. Part of the culture of the Internet is that you give back, that you post valuable information or utilities for the benefit of other people. Yet by posting PGP, Zimmerman got into serious trouble.

And there are lots of other similar cases—situations in which a cybernaut got into trouble by posting stuff. Right now, for example, two Californians are serving jail time basically for posting explicit pictures to adult **newsgroups**. Their pictures violated pornography laws in Tennessee, even though they posted the stuff in California.

continues

PGP *(continued)*

More than a few people have gotten into trouble by posting e-mail messages and newsgroup **articles** that made libelous statements about other people or companies.

So another lesson of the PGP story is that before you post anything anywhere, think carefully. You don't want to post something that violates a federal law or some obscure federal regulation. And you need to be careful, too, that you don't unwittingly break a local law in some other part of the country.

In a nutshell, how PGP works

How PGP works is sort of interesting. The whole encryption system relies on two keys, a public key and a private key. What you do (if you have PGP) is freely distribute the public key. Anyone who has PGP and your public key can use the public key to lock messages they send to you. Whenever you get a PGP-encrypted message, you unlock the message with the private key. The whole system works because, while anyone with the public key can lock a message, only a person with the correct private key can unlock it.

PINE   PINE is a popular **e-mail** software program developed, coincidentally, by my alma mater, the University of Washington. If you're connecting to the Internet using a **shell account** and the **HyperTerminal** application, for example, there's a good chance you're using PINE. (PINE has several hundred thousand users.) For this reason, I'm going to briefly describe how you send and read e-mail messages with PINE.

Starting PINE

Jeepers, this is actually the only tough part. I don't know how you start PINE with your **access provider**. If you see a menu when you connect and one of the choices is Mail or something like that, you simply choose that option. If you get a command prompt instead of a menu (this is what my access provider does), you probably type *pine*.

Once PINE starts, you'll see this opening menu or one that looks a lot like it.

Sending an E-Mail Message

To send an e-mail message, select the Compose Message option. You can do this by pressing the letter C. Or you can highlight the Compose Message option by pressing the P and N keys (which work like the Up and Down arrow keys, respectively) and then pressing Enter. When you do, PINE displays the Compose Message screen. Enter the name of the recipient or recipients first. Then press Enter to move to the next input blank. When you've addressed and entered the e-mail message, press Ctrl+X to send it. PINE will ask you to confirm that you want to send the message. Press *Y* for Yes to indicate you do.

Enter the Internet address of the person here.

Enter the Internet address of anyone who should receive a copy here.

Describe the message's content here.

Enter your message text by typing.

continues

P

PINE *(continued)*

A tip for new users of PINE

PINE, like many character-based **UNIX** programs, gives a list of command
keys at the bottom of the screen. The caret symbol (^) signifies the Ctrl
key. So you can press Ctrl+T, for example, to spell-check your message. If
you can't see these command keys, you can scroll the HyperTerminal window.

Reading an E-Mail Message

To read an e-mail message, select the Folder Index option. You can do
this by pressing the letter I. Or you can highlight the Folder Index
option by pressing the P and N keys as Up and Down arrow keys while
in the Main menu, and then press Enter. When you do, PINE displays
the Folder Index screen.

The Folder Index screen
just lists any e-mail
messages you've
received.

To read an e-mail
message, highlight it (by
using the P and N keys)
and then press Enter.

Once you select an e-mail
message from the Folder
Index screen, PINE
displays it in a Message
Text screen. Use the
spacebar and the hyphen
keys to move forward and
backward.

To delete the message,
press D.

To return to the main
PINE menu, press M.

Quitting PINE

To quit PINE, select the Quit option from the main menu. You can do this by pressing the letter Q. Or you can highlight the Quit option by pressing the P and N keys and then pressing Enter. PINE will ask if you really want to quit. Press Y for Yes.

Another couple of tips about PINE

PINE may look a little clumsy if you're used to working with Windows 95. But don't underestimate its usefulness. It's a very powerful e-mail utility. If you keep your eyes peeled and read the cryptic command descriptions at the bottom of each screen, you'll start to get a feel for what the utility can do. (I mentioned only a few of the commands here.) If you want more information about PINE, you may also want to know about the **FTP** and **World Wide Web** sites that the University of Washington maintains for people who want to know more: *ftp:// ftp.cac.washington.edu/pine* and *http://www/cac.washington.edu/pine*.

Ping

Remember that game the neighbor kids played when you were a kid? The one where you run up to someone's door, ring the bell, and then run away? Well, that's sort of what Ping does. In effect, Ping rings the doorbell of an Internet **host** to see if the Internet host will answer. Then it runs away. With Ping, however, this doorbell ringing business isn't just for fun. By pinging a host, you can tell whether it will respond. In fact, if you're trying to connect to a host but can't, you can try pinging the host. If you can't successfully ping the host, it probably means that the host is either shut down or is not responding to anything, or that a part of the Internet between you and this other host is shut down.

Using Ping

To use Ping, follow these steps:

1 Start MS-DOS. One way to do this is to click Start and then choose Programs and MS-DOS.

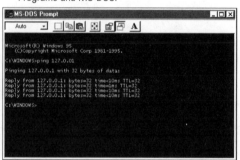

2 Change to the Windows directory, since this is where the Ping client is probably stored.

3 Type *ping* at the MS-DOS prompt followed by the **IP Address** of the host you want to ping.

More on Ping

If you type the PING command but don't include an IP address, Ping lists a bunch of command parameters you can enter after the IP address to control the way Ping pings.

The Loopback address

There's a loopback IP address, 127.0.0.1, that you should always be able to ping. That's because, for the purposes of Ping, your computer's IP address is 127.0.0.1. I mention this only because you'll sometimes see a nasty little joke in play on the Internet. Some **newbie** can't seem to connect. So somebody tells the newbie to ping the IP address 127.0.0.1 "just to see if you're really connected to the Internet." The newbie can of course ping 127.0.0.1, since that's his or her machine. And by this time the newbie is totally confused. "Gee," the newbie thinks, "Ping says I'm connected, but I can't seem to do anything...." And so it goes, with everyone getting a good laugh at the newbie's expense.

PPP

PPP stands for point-to-point protocol. It describes a method of connecting to the Internet in which your PC, for the duration of the connection, becomes a **host** computer on the Internet. The advantage of a PPP connection is that it simplifies the business of **downloading** and **uploading files,** as compared to just having a **shell account** with an **access provider**. With a PPP connection, you can move **files** directly between another host and your PC. (If you just use a shell account, you first move a file from some other host to the access provider's computer, and then from the access provider's computer to your PC.) A PPP connection also lets you use a **Web browser** like the **Internet Explorer** to browse the **World Wide Web**. The only disadvantages of a PPP connection are that access providers usually charge more money for them and they are slightly more difficult to set up. (You either use the **Internet Setup Wizard** or **Dial-Up Networking** to make a PPP connection.)

⁘ **Downloading Files; SLIP**

Pirates   If you've read much of this book or you've surfed the Internet, you're not going to be surprised by what I say next: There's a dark side to the Internet. No, it's not that the technology is dehumanizing. Or that the Internet is a stepping stone on the path to some Orwellian future. The dark side stems from the "pirates." "Who are the pirates?" you ask. (Pirates are also known by another name, "crackers.") Good question. These are the guys who break into **host** computers and then do things like steal the information stored there or store their own information there. This maybe sounds innocuous, but it's really not. What they're sometimes stealing are things like people's credit card numbers. And what they're often storing are pornography or stolen software. I'm not sure that there's anything you (or I) can do about all this. But I think you should be aware that while most of the people you run into on the Internet are wonderful, there are a handful of dirtballs.

PKUNZIP ⁙ PKZIP

PKZIP   PKZIP is a popular compression utility. Basically, what it does is scrunch **files** so that they take less space. How compression utilities scrunch files is beyond the scope of our little discussion. But all cybernauts should understand the usefulness of compression utilities like PKZIP. Scrunching a file makes it easier to move the file around the Internet. That makes sense, right? A file that is 100KB in size, all other factors being equal, will take longer to **download** and **upload** than a file that is 20KB in size.

Where to Find PKZIP

PKZIP is a shareware product, so you can find it in a bunch of different places. You can find it in the anonymous FTP site: *ftp:// ftp.cyberspace.com/dos/utils*. Almost surely, some of your PC-owning friends have it. You see it sometimes in some of the FTP sites on the Internet. You see it as well in some of the binary **newsgroups**, such as *alt.binaries.utilities*.

If you want to acquire a licensed copy of the product—and you should, it's well worth it—you can just call the manufacturer, PKWARE, Inc., at (414) 354-8699 or fax them at (414) 354-8559.

Once you get the PKZIP and PKUNZIP utilities, copy them to your MS-DOS directory (if you have one of these) or to your Windows folder. (My guess is that the MS-DOS directory is named DOS and that the Windows 95 folder is named WINDOWS.) The goal here is to stick the PKZIP and the PKUNZIP utilities in folders that appear in your path. By doing this, you don't have to specify where the PKZIP or the PKUNZIP command is located when you use it. You just use it.

PKZIPing a File

PKZIP is an MS-DOS utility. So what you want to do first is start an MS-DOS session. You can do this by clicking the Start button and then choosing Programs and then MS-DOS Prompt. To PKZIP a file, type the command PKZIP, a new name for the compressed file you'll create, and the name of the file you want to compress (including its path if the file isn't in the current directory). For example, to compress a file named PICTURES.TXT and create a new, PKZIPed file named PICTURES.ZIP, type the following at the MS-DOS command prompt:

```
PKZIP PICTURES.ZIP PICTURES.TXT
```

If the utility isn't in your path or the file to be compressed isn't in the active directory, you need to include path names with the file names. For example, if you stuck the PKZIP utility in a folder named UTILS on your C drive and the PICTURES.TXT file is in another directory named PICS on your C drive, you would type the following command at the MS-DOS command prompt:

```
C:\UTILS\PKZIP PICTURES.ZIP C:\PICS\PICTURES.TXT
```

continues

PKZIP *(continued)*

PKUNZIPing a File

Uncompressing a file with the PKUNZIP utility works in a fashion similar to that of the PKZIP utility. Start an MS-DOS session. Then type PKUNZIP followed by the name of the zipped file. For example, if PKUNZIP is in a folder in your path and the PKZIPed file is in the active directory, type the following at the MS-DOS command prompt:

```
PKUNZIP PICTURES.ZIP
```

If the utility isn't in your path or the compressed file isn't in the active directory, you need to include path names with the file names. For example, if you stuck the PKZIP utility in a folder named UTILS on your C drive and the PICTURES.ZIP file is in another directory named PICS on your C drive, you would type the following command at the MS-DOS command prompt:

```
C:\UTILS\PKUNZIP C:\PICS\PICTURES.ZIP
```

The dirt on compression

The amount of compression you get with PKZIP (and any other file compression utility, for that matter) varies wildly because it depends on the type of file you're compressing. Sometimes, PKZIP doesn't reduce the size of a file very much at all. If you try to PKZIP a **GIF** file, for example, you'll often get no real compression. The same thing is true of a **JPEG** file. Other graphics file formats, however, scrunch to 1 or 2 percent of their original size. While compression can sometimes make files much, much smaller—and it's probably always something you should try—it doesn't always deliver a benefit.

 **Downloading Files**

Port   Sometimes, you need to specify a port number as part of the **uniform resource locator.** The port doesn't have anything to do with the serial or parallel ports your computer uses to connect to devices like **modems** and printers. Rather, a port specifies which connection your session uses to connect to the **server.** I should say that you probably won't ever have to worry about this port business. But if you see a uniform resource locator that looks like the one that follows, the number that gets tagged onto the end of everything else is the port number:

```
telnet://locis.loc.gov:3000
```

3000 is the port number. I just made up this uniform resource locator, by the way. So don't try to Telnet there.

Protocol   In the world of diplomacy, a "protocol" refers to the rules of etiquette and ceremony that diplomats and heads of state follow. For example, "Don't drink from your finger bowl" is a protocol.

In the world of computers, "protocol" refers to the rules that two computers use to communicate. For example, "Don't send me data faster than I can receive it" is a very basic computer protocol.

🐾 **HyperTerminal; IP; TCP/IP; Zmodem**

Resource When I first started reading about the Internet, I kept stumbling across the term *resource*. I found it really confusing. It finally dawned on me that people used the term to refer to a bunch of different things that were all sort of alike.

People sometimes use the term as a sort of catchall category to refer to an Internet service like a **newsgroup,** the **World Wide Web,** or **FTP.** Other times, the word refers to specific **servers**—mail servers, newsgroup servers, World Wide Web servers, **Gopher** servers, FTP servers, and so on. Still other times it refers to specific **files** (and their locations).

I think the most accurate way to use the term is to refer to something that can be described with a **uniform resource locator.** That's the way I use the term in this book. I use it to refer both to servers and to specific files. This is probably all crystal-clear to you now. And you're wondering why I had all the trouble in the first place.

ROT13 ROT13 is a code. People sometimes use it to encrypt messages that they don't want other people to read by mistake. For example, if you posted a message with information or commentary that was offensive to some people, you could encrypt the message using the ROT13 code. By doing this, you'd be in effect warning people, "Hey, there's some pretty crazy stuff in this message. You probably don't want to read it if you're easily offended."

The ROT13 code is easy to break, however. Anyone who really wants to can break the code and read a message that has been encrypted with the ROT13 code. In fact, The **Microsoft Network** includes a command, Tools Rot13, that you can use to encrypt and decrypt messages that have the ROT13 code. So anyone who wants to read a ROT13-encrypted message can probably decrypt the code. But because of the code, there is less chance of anyone accidentally reading the message.

This message has been encrypted using the ROT13 code.

```
Nsgre n pregnva cbvag, zbarl vf zrnavatyrff.
Vg prnfrf gb or gur tbny. Gur tnzr vf jung pbhagf.
    --Nevfgbgyr Banffvf
```

Here's the decrypted message. Pretty inflammatory, huh?

```
After a certain point, money is meaningless.
It ceases to be the goal. The game is what counts.
    --Aristotle Onassis
```

·:· Encryption

RTFM   You see this acronym in postings to **newbies** a lot. But I
wouldn't suggest using it unless you know what the letter
"F" stands for. The R, T, and M stand for "Read The
Manual."

Scripting   Some communications applications provide a scripting feature. In a nutshell, a scripting feature types stuff for
you. Your **username**, your **password**, and anything else
you're supposed to type as you make a connection. While
the **HyperTerminal** application doesn't provide such a
feature, the **Dial-Up Networking** application (which you
use to make **PPP** connections) does. To write a Dial-Up
Networking script, you use the Dial-Up Scripting Tool.
(To open this application, click the Start button, then
choose Programs, Accessories, and the Dial-Up Scripting
Tool.)

Server   When you use your PC to connect directly to another **host computer**—for example, when you use a **PPP** connection—your PC is called a **client**. The other host computer is a **server**. Since we're already on the topic, I may as well also say that the software that runs on the client is client software. And the software that runs on the server is—big surprise here—server software.

One thing that's good to remember is that to do just about anything, your client software and the server software need to work together. Oftentimes you can't accomplish some task, even though the client and its software work, because either the server or its software doesn't work.

Sex   There's a ton of sexually oriented material in Internet **newsgroups** such as *alt.sex.stories* and *alt.binaries.pictures.erotica*. There are also a handful of **World Wide Web** sites that offer sexual material, including *http://www.playboy.com* and *http://www.penthousemag.com*. Some of this stuff is tame and some is very explicit. Some of this stuff qualifies as art. And some of it is disgusting. (I think the disgusting stuff mostly appears in newsgroups without **moderators**. But I'm not sure. I have not done exhaustive research on this.)

⁚⁚ Free Speech

Shareware

Shareware is software that is given away free. If you like the software or intend to use it, you are supposed to send a small fee to the programmer who created it. Some shareware applications have code written into them that makes the programs inoperable unless users pay the fee within a certain period of time. Besides computer applications, clip art collections and font files are distributed as shareware. In fact, I think it's fair to say that the Internet's **FTP** sites and **newsgroups** are chock-full of shareware.

Freeware, a variation of shareware, is given away absolutely free. You don't have to send any money to the programmer who invented it, although most programmers ask for a postcard or some other gratis acknowledgment. I guess they want to know who's using their software.

Shell Account

With a shell account, you use a communications application like **HyperTerminal** to connect to an Internet **access provider.** Your PC becomes, in effect, just a monitor and keyboard attached to the access provider's **host computer.** Shell accounts are less expensive, usually, than the alternatives, **PPP** and **SLIP** connections.

⁘ Connections

Shortcut Icons

Windows 95 lets you place icons for commonly used documents, programs, **folders,** and other stuff like this on the **desktop.** This maybe doesn't seem like all that neat of a deal, but it is. By putting one of these icons, called shortcut icons, on the desktop, you can open a program like Internet Explorer or some other Internet client with a simple double-click. (The **Internet Setup Wizard** adds a shortcut icon for the **Internet Explorer** to the desktop. But you may want to add shortcut icons for other client software programs, such as **FTP** and **Telnet.**)

This is a shortcut icon. Windows uses an icon that identifies the application it will instruct to open the program—in this case, the Telnet **client.**

Creating a Shortcut Icon

To create a shortcut icon for an Internet **client** like FTP or Telnet, follow these steps:

1 Start **Windows Explorer.**

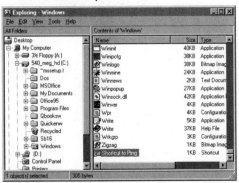

2 Select the client, or program, for which you want to create the shortcut icon. (You may need to select the **folder** that holds the client first.)

3 Choose the File Create Shortcut command. Windows Explorer adds a shortcut to the folder.

4 Drag the shortcut to the desktop. Windows Explorer moves the shortcut icon to the desktop.

Shouting If you type an **e-mail** message or a **newsgroup** article in all capital letters, it's called shouting. BUT YOU SHOULDN'T DO THIS. IT'S ANNOYING AS ALL GET OUT. What's more, type in all capital letters is hard to read.

Netiquette

Signature A signature is just an extra little bit of text you attach to the end of every **e-mail** message you send. If you use **Microsoft Exchange** as your e-mail program and WordMail as your e-mail editor, you can add signatures to your e-mail messages using Microsoft Word's AutoText feature. If you use an **access provider's** e-mail program, you can usually create a signature file that the e-mail program automatically tags onto the end of your e-mail messages.

Sometimes people use signatures to share a pithy quotation. Sometimes people use them to provide their full name and address or something like that. Don't use a signature to sell anything. You'll probably violate a bunch of **netiquette** rules and find yourself subjected to endless **flames**.

SLIP SLIP stands for serial line internet protocol. Like **PPP**, it is a method of directly connecting to the Internet. When you make a SLIP connection, your PC becomes a **host computer** on the Internet for the duration of the connection. The advantage of a SLIP connection (and a PPP connection) is that it simplifies the business of **downloading** and **uploading files**, as compared to a **shell account** connection. With a SLIP or PPP connection, you only have to move a file once (from the host that acts as the **server** to your PC), rather than twice (first from the host that acts as the server to the **access provider's** computer, and then from the access provider's computer to your PC).

A SLIP connection also lets you do things like browse the **World Wide Web**. The only two disadvantages of a SLIP connection are that access providers usually charge more money for them and they are slightly more difficult to set up. (You use the **Dial-Up Networking** program to make a SLIP connection.)

S

SLIP vs. PPP

If you have a choice between a PPP or SLIP connection, choose PPP. PPP is pretty much the standard these days. Plus, PPP is faster than SLIP. What's more, it's easier to set up a PPP connection. No matter how you got Windows 95 on your machine, you have all the stuff you need already. (The SLIP stuff comes only on the CD version of Windows 95.) Finally, some of the stuff you have to do to set up a SLIP connection is rather complicated. You have to worry about **IP** header compression, for example. Yuck.

 Downloading Files

Smileys E-mail, like any writing, isn't a very precise communication tool. It's easy to say too much. Or too little. Or to leave the reader confused or angry. And all of this stuff is true even if you're the world's greatest living novelist (or so I imagine). To deal with the limitations of the written word in **e-mail,** people sometimes add smileys, also called emoticons, to their messages. In essence, a smiley is a face you make with symbol keys. For example, by combining the colon with the end parenthesis mark—turn the page sideways to see this—you get a smiley face. Sort of.

:)

And if you combine the colon with the begin parenthesis mark, you get a frowning face:

: (

Lots of people—and you may be one—find it helpful to use these faces to say what their prose doesn't say. Do smileys work? I don't know. You be the judge:

Sue,

I'm sorry I missed you.

I thought we had a date. But I guess not.

See you around the playground.

Steve

: (

Snail Mail

Snail mail is what **cybernauts** sometimes call the regular mail. You know, the kind with letters, envelopes, stamps, and letter carriers. The name slams the postal service for its slowness. Even if the postal service didn't lose letters or deliver them slowly, however, snail mail would still be slow compared to electronic mail, which can move a message around the world in a matter of seconds. (I should probably tell you, however, that **e-mail** isn't always this fast. Sometimes an e-mail message can take hours to reach its destination.)

Spam

First of all, I don't know why Spam—the ham-derived meat product—gets such a bad rap. When I was a kid going to summer camp, they fed us Spam, pancakes, burnt toast, and scrambled eggs. Every morning. And the Spam wasn't the worst item on the menu. No way. And here's the other thing I always wonder about: When we use the term in a derogatory, inside-joke manner, are we making fun of people who can't afford to spend more for food? Okay, I'll stop talking about this angle on the Spam question now. But you catch my drift.

A joke we can't pass up

Descartes said, "I think therefore I am." Hormel said, "I'm pink therefore I'm Spam."

Let's get back to the Internet. I need to tell you what Spam has to do with cyberspace. If you post the same message to a bunch of different **newsgroups**, it's called spamming. And it's considered bad form. (By the way, a Velveeta is similar to a spam: It's a newsgroup posting, often commercial in nature, that is excessively cross-posted to a large number of newsgroups.)

Flame; Netiquette

Subfolder I'm using the term subfolder to refer to a **folder** within a folder. This isn't some technical term I learned over at Microsoft, by the way. I just made it up.

Switching Tasks To switch tasks in Windows 95, use the Taskbar. The Taskbar is the bar along the bottom of the screen. It shows the Start button on the left side. To the right of the Start button are buttons that represent applications that are open.

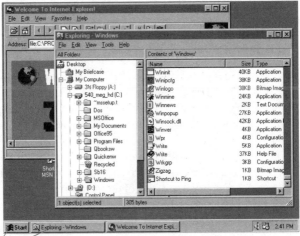

To switch to an application that is open, click its button.

To open a new program, use the Start button. With Windows 95, you can run several applications at the same time.

⁛ Multitasking

T1 Transmission Line
A T1 transmission line connects host computers and passes information at a rate of 1.5Mbps. That's pretty fast. Sometimes letters and abbreviations like Mbps confuse people. So let's look at all of this in a table without the kooky acronyms.

The lingo	Transmission speed
2400bps modem	2,400 **bits** (1s or 0s) per second
14.4K modem	14,400 **bits per second**
1.5Mbps T1 line	1,500,000 bits per second
45Mbps T3 line	45,000,000 bits per second

When I first heard about T1 transmission lines, I thought I needed one. Bad. Partly for the **bandwidth.** But also because my brother has one (he does research at a university). Alas, I soon learned that T1 lines are very, very expensive. Even if you have a short connection to make to another nearby **host computer,** you'll pay at least several hundred dollars a month—and very possibly a couple of thousand dollars a month. If you have a long connection to make to a faraway host computer, you could pay thousands of dollars a month. (One major aerospace company gets by with a single T1 line at a cost of $20,000 a month, for example.) So I don't have a T1 transmission line.

High bandwidth doesn't always equal high performance

Many otherwise sophisticated people share a common misconception concerning those high-bandwidth transmission lines I just mentioned. Because the Internet is a **packet switched network**, if you have a T1 transmission line, you quite likely share your transmission line with a bunch of other people. And because you share it, it may be that rather than personally moving 1.5Mbps on a T1 transmission line, you and nine of your fellow users simultaneously move data at a perceived rate of roughly 150Kbps. Or maybe you and 99 of your fellow users simultaneously move data at a perceived rate of roughly 15Kbps. Collectively, you guys are moving 1.5Mbps. But no one user gets all the bandwidth. This whole confusion, by the way, stems from the fact that people think the Internet works like a **circuit switched network,** which it doesn't.

Baud

T3 Transmission Line
A T3 transmission line moves data at a rate of 45Mbps. That's really fast. In fact, the old **NSFNET** backbone used T3 transmission lines. And **online services** such as The **Microsoft Network** use T3 transmission lines as well.

☙ **T1 Transmission Line**

TCP/IP
TCP/IP is the **protocol** that describes how information gets passed around the Internet. (A protocol is essentially a bunch of rules.) TCP/IP breaks information into **packets,** routes those packets from the sending computer to the receiving computer, and finally reassembles the packets once they reach the receiving computer. If a packet is missing—say it gets lost somewhere on its trip from the sending computer—TCP/IP directs the sending computer to send another copy of the missing packet.

TCP/IP stands for Transmission Control Protocol/Internet Protocol, if you care to know, and I wouldn't blame you if you didn't.

☙ **Gulf War**

Telnet   When you Telnet, you **log in** to another computer or **net-work.** Okay. This sounds kooky, I know. But say you're logged in to an **access provider's** computer or network. And you've been noodling around. Using a Telnet command, you can probably log in to another computer network. In other words, even if you are 5,000 miles away from the computer or network you want to log in to, you can use the Internet to make the connection. How Telnet connections work depends on whether you have a **shell account** connection or a **PPP** or **SLIP** connection. (You can't Telnet from an **online service** like The **Microsoft Network.**) I'll describe the mechanics of Telnetting using both the shell account and PPP or SLIP connection methods by describing how you can connect to the U.S Library of Congress's LOCIS system.

Telnetting with a Shell Account

To Telnet with a shell account, first you need to make the connection by using **HyperTerminal** or some other communications application. Once you've done this, you need to issue the *telnet* command and specify the Telnet site. How you do this depends on your access provider's system. The access provider may provide a menu. Or you may simply type the command *telnet* followed by the Telnet site's **host** and **domain name.** Then you press Enter.

This is the way the HyperTerminal window looks when I'm about to Telnet to LOCIS.

What you see next is the logon screen for the Telnet site. It may ask you for a **username** (or user ID) and a **password**. The convention is to type the word *anonymous* as the username, press Enter, type your Internet **e-mail** name as the password, and press Enter again.

Once you've logged in to the Telnet site, you're set. You'll see whatever anyone else sees when they log on to the computer or network. In the case of the LOCIS Telnet site, for example, you get a menu of numbered options. To select an option, you type its number.

Telnetting with a PPP or SLIP Connection and the Telnet Client

Windows 95 comes with a Telnet client. To use it, you start the Telnet client using the **Windows Explorer.** The Telnet client probably is located in the Windows **folder.** (If you plan to use Telnet very much, you can save time by adding a **shortcut icon** for the Telnet client to your **desktop.**)

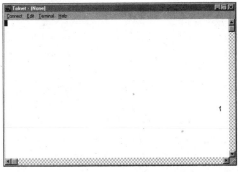

continues

Telnet *(continued)*

To make your Telnet connection once you've started Telnet, follow
these steps:

1 Choose the Connect Remote System command. (If you haven't yet
connected to your access provider, this is when Windows 95
makes the PPP connection.)

2 Enter the **host name** for the Telnet site in the Host Name drop-
down list box.

3 If necessary, enter the Telnet **port** number in the Port drop-down
list box.

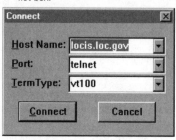

4 If necessary, specify a terminal emulation type by using the
TermType drop-down list box.

5 Click Connect. Telnet makes the connection. Next, you see either
the login screen for the Telnet site (it asks for a username or user
ID and a password), or you see the main menu if there isn't a for-
mal login.

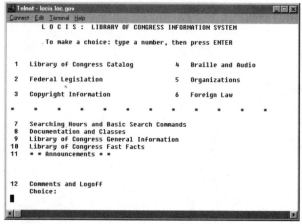

☙ **Port; Troubleshooting: Telnet; Quick Reference: Telnet
Command Guide**

Terminal Terminal was the old Windows 3.x communications application. You won't need or want to use Terminal anymore. You'll want to use **HyperTerminal** instead. HyperTerminal is much, much faster.

Thread As you might know, the messages that people post to **newsgroups** are called **articles.** You might also know that people can post articles that respond to other articles. The original article that someone posts along with any responses that other people post is called a thread.

TIN TIN is a **newsgroup** reader that many **access providers** give to people with **shell accounts.** Because of its popularity, I'm going to describe how to use it to read and post newsgroup **articles.** I'll also describe how to use to it **encode** articles and unencode encoded articles—such as those articles that are actually encoded pictures or software programs.

continues

TIN *(continued)*

Starting TIN

Your access provider may have a menu that lets you read and post to **newsgroups** (or **USENET newsgroups**, as they may call them). In this case, you just select the newsgroups or USENET News command and away you go.

If there isn't a newsgroups or USENET News command menu—and often even if there is one—you can usually type *tin* at the command prompt.

As TIN starts, you may get some messages asking if you want to subscribe to new newsgroups or remove old, unused, or bogus newsgroups. Answer these questions by pressing *Y* for Yes or *N* for No. (You can also press *Q* or *q* to quit if you don't want to answer any questions without your attorney present.) TIN next builds a list, or index, of newsgroups and displays the first part of this list on your monitor.

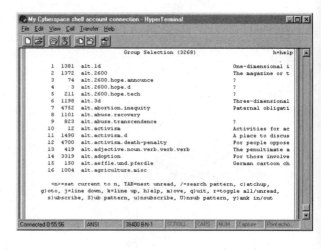

Finding the Newsgroup You Want

To find the newsgroup you want, simply page through the list. Press *J* or *K* to move forward or backward one newsgroup at a time. Or press *Ctrl+D* or *Ctrl+U* to move forward and backward a page at a time. Once you find the newsgroup you want, press Enter. This tells TIN to list the articles posted to the newsgroup you selected.

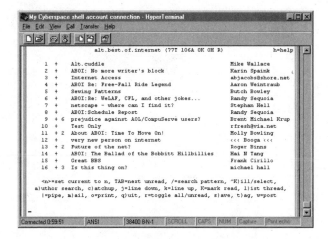

By the way, there are thousands and thousands of newsgroups. You need to do a bit of searching to find the ones that interest you. As a start, you may want to focus on newsgroups that have a lot of activity (since this may signal that a fair number of people find the newsgroup interesting) or on moderated newsgroups. (As the **moderator** entry explains, a moderated newsgroup is one where someone moderates, or polices, the newsgroup so that a bunch of stupid stuff isn't posted by goofballs, dingbats, red techs, and other riffraff.)

So what's a red tech? Just for the record, a red tech is an Internet-surfing, high-tech redneck. The term "red tech" was first coined by Peter X. Weverka, a notorious computer book editor.

continues

T

TIN *(continued)*

Reading Articles in a Newsgroup

To read an article, first page through the list to find one that sounds interesting. As with paging through the index of newsgroups, press *J* or *K* to move forward or backward one newsgroup article at a time. Or press *Ctrl+D* or *Ctrl+U* to move forward or backward a page at a time. Once you find the article you want, press Enter. This tells TIN to display the article.

This is the first page of an article posted to the *alt.best.of.internet* newsgroup.

Saving a Single Article

To save an article you're reading, press *Q* to return to the index. Make sure the article you want is the one selected. (You may need to press *J* or *K* to select the next or previous article.) Then, press *S* to indicate you want to save the article. TIN asks what you want to save. Press *A* to indicate you want to save the article. When prompted, enter a **file name** for your article and then press Enter.

TIN next asks if you want anything special done to the article you're saving before it's actually saved. If you're saving an article—just a bunch of text you want to keep as text—press *N* for No. If you're saving a picture or a software utility that has been encoded but needs to be unencoded, press *U*. TIN, with the help of the access provider's computer, will do its thing. When TIN finishes unencoding the article (if you've told it to unencode), it asks if it should delete any "post processing" files. Press *N* for No. Now TIN redisplays the list of articles for the newsgroup.

Saving a Tagged Set of Articles

There's a physical limit to the size of an article. For this reason, large files that get encoded as text and are then posted—such as pictures and software utilities—get posted as a set of articles rather than just one article. For example, a set of articles that combine to form a big financial utility named, say, FINCALC.EXE, may be listed in the following way:

FINCALC.EXE (1/4)

FINCALC.EXE (2/4)

FINCALC.EXE (3/4)

FINCALC.EXE (4/4)

To save and decode this set of articles together, you need to do a little extra work. First, you need to tag, or number, the articles in the correct order. To do this, select the first article and press *T*. Then select the second article, press *T;* select the third article, press *T;* and so on. Articles aren't always listed in the same order as they need to be tagged, or numbered. Sometimes you need to do a bit of jumping around.

Once you've tagged the articles in the set, you're ready to save them. First, press *S* to indicate you want to save the tagged articles. TIN asks what you want to save. Press *T* to indicate you want to save the tagged articles. When prompted, enter a file name for the set of tagged articles and then press Enter. TIN next asks if you want anything special done to the article you're saving before it's actually saved. If you're saving an article—just a bunch of text you want to keep as text—press *N* for No.

If you're saving a picture or a software utility that has been encoded but needs to be uudecoded, press *U*. TIN, with the help of the access provider's computer, will do its thing. When TIN finishes uudecoding the article, it asks if it should delete "post processing" files. Press *Y* for Yes. TIN next redisplays the list of articles for the newsgroup.

Let me quickly tell you one more thing. In the case of binary files, you sometimes see a first article labeled something like "part 0 of 4," or simply (0/4). For example, in the list of articles given earlier, the first article might be FINCALC.EXE (0/4). In this case, FINCALC.EXE (0/4) is really just a description of the other articles. You would not tag and save this file because it's not part of the binary file.

continues

TIN *(continued)*

Posting Articles

To post an article with TIN, first display the newsgroup to which you want to post the article. Then follow these steps:

1 Press *W*.

2 When prompted with the "Post subject" question, enter a brief description of your article.

3 Press Enter. TIN displays a screen that asks you for some information about the posted article, including a summary description.

4 Type your message.

5 Press *Ctrl+X*.

6 When TIN asks if you want to save your article, type *Y* or *y* to indicate you do.

7 When TIN asks which file name to use for your message, press Enter to accept the suggested file name.

8 When asked whether you want to quit, edit, or post your message, press *P* for "post." TIN posts your message.

Posting Binary Files

To post a binary file with TIN, you follow almost the same set of steps as you do for posting a regular old message:

1 Press *W*.

2 When prompted with the "Post subject" question, enter a brief description of your binary file.

3 Press Enter. TIN displays a screen that asks you for some information about the article, including a summary description.

4 Type a brief message.

5 Press *Ctrl+R*. TIN prompts you for the name of the binary file you want to post. (If you don't know the file name or it isn't in the current directory, you can press *Ctrl+T* to display a list of the files and directories in the current directory. You can use the arrow keys to select the directory and the file.) Once you select the file, TIN encodes it if necessary.

6 Press *Ctrl+X*.

7 TIN asks if you want to save the answer in the modified buffer, or something like that. Answer by pressing *Y*.

8 TIN asks you something about what name to use for saving the article. Just press Enter.

9 When asked whether you want to quit, edit, or post your message, press *P* for "post." TIN posts your message.

Want to test out this posting business?

The busiest newsgroup you'll see is *alt.test*. It's the one you use to test whether your posting technique works. If you want to try out the steps I've described here, post to *alt.test*. To see if your message posted correctly, check that newsgroup in an hour or so (or check it tomorrow). By the way, you'll get automatic **e-mail** responses from some of the **NNTP** sites that maintain the *alt.test* newsgroup. They send responses so you know your message got posted. If you don't want to see any of these responses, include the word "ignore" in your message header.

 Encoded Files; Downloading Files; Uploading Files

Uniform Resource Locator

The uniform resource locator, or URL, specifies how you find an Internet **resource.** There are really four parts to a uniform resource locator: the service or **protocol;** the **server** name; the path; and the document, or file, name.

A Sample URL Explained

Let me explain what each of these things is, using a real-life Web page—the one that provides biographical data on the President of the United States and his family.

`http://www.whitehouse.gov/White_House/html/Life.html.`

http:// identifies this resource as part of the **World Wide Web.**

www.whitehouse.gov/ identifies the server. (Notice that whitehouse.gov is really a **domain name.**)

White_House/html/ names the directory and subdirectory with the World Wide Web document.

Life.html names the World Wide Web document.

Reviewing the Other Services and Protocols

The World Wide Web is only one of the services available on the Internet. Not surprisingly then, URLs use other codes to identify the other services and protocols. Here's a list of codes with some examples and additional comments:

Service or protocol	Explanation
file://	Refers either to the file transfer protocol or to a way to access a file on the local computer.
ftp://	Refers to the file transfer protocol.
gopher://	Refers to the **Gopher** service.
http://	Refers to the HyperText Transfer Protocol (**HTTP**), which is what you use to browse the World Wide Web.
news://	Refers to the network news transfer protocol, which is what you use to browse **newsgroups**.
telnet://	Used to start a **Telnet** session.

The URL blues

You can make a couple of easy mistakes when it comes to URLs. One is to mistakenly use backward slashes (\) instead of forward slashes (/). For example, the correct URL is *http://www.microsoft.com/*, not *http:\\www.microsoft.com* . The other easy mistake concerns case. **UNIX** operating systems recognize case (lower vs. upper) in file names although not in server names. So if the URL is *http://www.blah.com/file.html* and you enter *http://www.blah.com/FILE.HTML*, it probably won't work. Note, however, that the URLs *http://www.blah.com/file.html* and *http://WWW.BLAH.COM/file.html* are equivalent. In other words, case doesn't matter for the server name. Let me say one last thing. You'll usually be fine if you use all lowercase letters.

 HTML

UNIX

If you're going to surf the Internet, you'll come into frequent contract with UNIX because many Internet **hosts** use UNIX. So I'm going to give you quick descriptions of a handful of common UNIX commands.

Note, however, that *many* different "flavors" of UNIX systems are used out there. I've tried to stick with the most common commands, but if you run into trouble, you may need to use the UNIX *man* command ("man" stands for "manual") to make sure some of the less common commands work on the machine you are connected to. (The *man* command is also a good way to see some of the additional commands and flags that are available.)

Command	Description
^C *or* **^X** (Ctrl+C *or* Ctrl+X)	These commands stop UNIX while it is performing a command. If I accidentally asked UNIX to list all of the directories and subdirectories on the host computer, it could take hours, so I might use these commands to interrupt the computer and tell it to stop. (Note: Because computers are so fast at processing these commands, it could take a while for the output on the monitor to catch up to the work the computer has done. It will look as though the commands haven't affected anything, even though the computer has already stopped. Be patient.)
apropos *word*	Looks through the manual and gives you every instance of the word you ask for. Use it if you're not sure what you're looking for.
cd *directoryname*	Changes the working directory to the specified directory.
ls *filename* or *directoryname*	Displays a **file name** or the contents of a directory, *except* any files beginning with a period ("dot"). These are special configuration files, such as .SIGNATURE, .CSHRC, .LOGOUT, etc. If you don't specify a file name or directory name, the command shows the contents of the current directory.

Command	Description
ls -a	Lists all of the files in the current directory, *including* those that begin with a dot.
ls -C *directoryname*	Lists all the files in a multicolumn format, instead of one name to a line. The number of columns is set automatically by the system. (You can change the number of columns, but doing so is very complicated.)
ls -F	Displays a slash (/) after the name if it's a directory, and an asterisk (*) after the name if it can be executed (like a program). A few other signs are used for other types of files.
ls -R	Displays the names of any files, directories, subdirectories, sub-subdirectories, and so on, related to the work directory.
man *command*	Lists the help information for the command. ("Man" stands for "manual," so you can think of this as the host computer "help file.")
rm *filename*	Deletes the file from the UNIX host. The wildcards that are used for the MS-DOS DEL command may also be used here.
rm -i *filespecification*	When trying to delete more than one file, the -i flag tells the computer to ask whether you really want to delete the file before it deletes it. This is a great precaution to take, particularly if you're not comfortable with UNIX yet.
rm -r *directoryname*	Removes directories and their contents, including all subdirectories. In the beginning, it might be wise to combine this flag with the -i flag so that you are prompted at every stage of file and directory deletion.
rz *filename*	Used when you want the host computer to receive a file you are sending from your computer.
rz -b *filename*	Receives the file from you in binary format.
rz -p *filename*	Receives the file only if there is no file by that name in the receiving directory. The -p, or protect, flag keeps UNIX from overwriting a file you already have.

continues

UNIX *(continued)*

Command	Description
sz *filename*	Sends the file from the host computer or program to your computer, using **Zmodem**. Windows 95 automatically receives the file. The MS-DOS file name wildcards ? and * may also be used to receive multiple files.
sz -e *filename*	Sends the file to you, replacing all control characters with **escape characters.**
sz -b *filename*	Sends the file in binary format. Sometimes, if you're having problems sending or receiving a file, using this flag can help solve them.
sz -n *filename*	Sends the file only if there is no file by that name in the receiving directory. Also sends the file if there is a file by that name, but the file being sent is newer, in which case the file being sent replaces the old file.
sz -p *filename*	Sends the file only if there is no file by that name in the receiving directory. This keeps UNIX from overwriting a file you already have.

About the command flags

The *ls* flags may be combined. For example, my standard command for seeing what's in a directory is *ls -Fa*. That way, I can see all of the files in the directory, including dot files, and I can tell whether they're "special" files or "regular" files. The rz and sz flags can also be combined. For instance, suppose you wanted to receive all files with a DOC extension in binary format, but receive them only if files with the same name did not already exist in the receiving directory. In this case, you would enter *sz -bp *.doc*. You must use the correct case with each flag.

HyperTerminal; Shell Account

Uploading Files
How you move a **file** from your PC to the Internet depends on the way you've connected to the Internet. If you've connected with a **shell account** and what you want to do is move a file to your **access provider**—perhaps so you can post it to a **newsgroup**—you use a communications application like **HyperTerminal**. If you've connected with a **PPP** or **SLIP** connection, you don't need to move a file from your PC to the Internet because your PC is already part of the Internet. With a PPP or SLIP connection, you can move the file using Windows 95's **FTP client**. If you're using an **online service** like The **Microsoft Network**, you use whatever commands the online service's client software provides.

Downloading Files

URL Uniform Resource Locator

UseNet Newsgroups Newsgroups

Username
When you **log in** to a **network,** the network wants to know your identity. To identify yourself, give your name or username. Your username is also the first part of your Internet **e-mail** address.

Authentication; Internet Explorer; TIN

Viewer   To look at a graphics file such as a **GIF** or **JPEG** file, or to look at a movie file such as an **MPEG** file or AVI file, you need a viewer. A viewer is just a program that opens graphics files and movie files. Windows 95 comes with a viewer that lets you look at AVI files, the Multimedia Player. The **Internet Explorer** comes with an internal viewer that lets you look at GIF and JPEG files. To open an MPEG file, you need an MPEG viewer.

You can often find **shareware** and freeware viewers in the *alt.binaries.utilities* **newsgroup**. To use one of these viewers, you first need to decode it and then **download** it.

❖ **Encoded Files**

Virus   A virus is a program created by a pathetic little wimp with a bit of technical knowledge but zero maturity, zero common sense, and zero morals. The virus program this loser creates often attempts to destroy either your computer or the data stored on your computer's hard disk.

You get viruses by using infected floppy disks or infected software on your computer. You also get viruses by **downloading** infected **files** from the Internet.

If your machine does get a virus or if you're wondering whether your machine has one, you can probably locate and eradicate it by using an anti-virus program. You can usually get an anti-virus program in any of the popular system utilities sets such as Norton Utilities from Semantec or PC Tools Deluxe from Central Point Software.

VT100   Many years ago, Digital Equipment Corporation, a computer hardware manufacturer, created a terminal called the VT100. Because this terminal was so popular, it became a sort of de facto terminal standard. As a result, many terminals (and personal computers that emulate terminals) must pretend to be VT100s when they connect to **BBSs** (bulletin board systems) and Internet **access providers.**

If you're connected to the Internet by way of an access provider and the access provider wants your personal computer to pretend that it's a VT100 terminal, start **HyperTerminal.** Then, once it's running, choose the File Properties command.

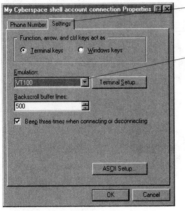

Click the Settings tab to see the terminal emulation options.

Choose the VT100 entry from the Emulation list box.

W³ ⁘ World Wide Web

WAIS

WAIS stands for Wide Area Information Service. But you don't really need to know that. What you should know is that WAIS, pronounced "ways," works sort of like **Gopher**. Using a WAIS **client** running on your PC or on your **access provider's** computer, you search through indexes of topics maintained by WAIS **servers**. Typically, conducting a WAIS search takes at least two steps. The first step is to identify a handful of WAIS servers that provide indexes covering the subject matter you're curious about. The second step is to search through the indexes of these WAIS servers for whatever bit of information you need. Neither Windows 95 nor Plus! for Windows 95 comes with a WAIS client. So I won't go into a bunch more detail here. If you want to use the Internet to do research and data gathering, however, you should definitely learn more about WAIS. Check with your access provider first. If your provider doesn't have a WAIS client with decent documentation, purchase one of the larger books on surfing the Internet to learn about WAIS.

WAN

Do network acronyms never stop? I guess not. WAN stands for wide area network, as in a **network** that includes computers across the state, province, shire, or country.

🐾 **LAN; MAN**

Web 🐾 **World Wide Web**

White Pages White pages are like electronic address books. You can use white pages to look up someone's **e-mail** address or even their real address and telephone number. Some white pages can be searched using **Gopher**.

Wildcard Characters Wildcard characters stand in for other characters in an expression. For example, you can use wildcard characters to stand in for characters in a **file name** when you're searching for a **file**, and you can use them as part of a command. The most common wildcard characters are the ? and * symbols. A ? can stand for any single character. An * can stand for any single character, any group of characters, or for no group of characters at all. For example, if you are connected to an **access provider** that runs **UNIX** on its computer and you want to send all of the files in a directory using the send **Zmodem** command *sz*, you could type:

```
sz  *
```

Windows Explorer

Windows Explorer lets you do things: It lets you view and work with your computer's disks and the **files** that are stored on your disk. It also lets you view and work with the other parts of your computer—its fonts, Control Panel, and your printers. What's more, you can also use Windows Explorer to work with The **Microsoft Network**.

Starting Windows Explorer

To start Windows Explorer, click the Start button. Then choose Programs and Windows Explorer. The Windows Explorer window appears.

Windows Explorer uses a **folder pane** to show the **folder** structure.

Windows Explorer uses a **file pane** to show the **subfolders** and the files in the active folder. Windows Explorer provides file information, including the file size in **kilobytes** and the last modification date. (The last modification date is the date someone last fiddled with the file by changing its contents.)

Selecting Disks

To select a disk, click on the disk icon in the folder pane.

Selecting Folders

To select a folder, scroll through the folder pane until you see the folder you want. Then click the folder.

If the folder is a subfolder in another folder, you may need to first select the parent folder and display its subfolder. You can do this by clicking the parent folder.

W

Windows Explorer alerts you to subfolders

Windows Explorer adds the plus sign (+) to a folder icon if the folder it represents has subfolders.

Selecting Files

To select a file in the active folder, scroll through the file pane until you see the file. Then click it.

You can select more than one file at once by clicking on the first file, holding down Shift, and then clicking on the last file. Or you can hold down Ctrl and click each file you want to select.

Opening Files

To open a file in the active folder, scroll through the file pane until you see the application or document. Then double-click the file. When you double-click an application, Windows 95 starts the application. When you double-click a document, Windows 95 starts the application in which the document was created and tells the application to open the document you clicked.

WordPad WordPad is the built-in word processor that comes with Windows 95. I'm not going to tell you how you use this handy little application. Mostly, you just use the keyboard to enter text into a window that appears in the middle of your screen. I did want to remind you (or alert you) that WordPad is available. If you start collecting ASCII text files—maybe you've been **FTPing** a bunch— you'll need a way to view and print the files. And WordPad will do these things nicely.

Is there anything else I should tell you about WordPad? Oh yes, you can start WordPad by clicking the Start button and then choosing Programs, Accessories, and WordPad. Once WordPad is up and running, you can open an ASCII text file by choosing the File Open command and then selecting the file. And you can print by choosing the File Print command.

World Wide Web   The World Wide Web (also known as W^3, the Web, and WWW) is just a set of multimedia documents that are connected so you can jump from one document to another by way of hypertext links, usually with a click. If this definition sounds complicated, it's probably because I've used a handful of terms I shouldn't have: document, multimedia, and hypertext. But let me define these terms for you and make the whole picture pretty clear.

This is the White House's World Wide Web document.

Let's start with the key term, document. A document is just a little report that describes something. Often, documents are on paper. In fact, you've probably created hundreds of paper documents: book reports in grade school; thank-you letters to distant, gift-giving relatives; and perhaps lengthy term papers in college. You wrote these documents on paper, but if you had produced and displayed them on a computer screen, they still would have been documents, right? So now you know what I mean by document.

The multimedia part relates to the fact that when you create and display a document on a computer, you aren't limited to words. You can place pictures in a document, for example. And you can place sound objects. (A World Wide Web document from the Office of the President of the United States has Socks the cat's meow in it: *http:// www.whitehouse.gov/White_House/html/Life.html.*) Just about any object a computer can create, display, or play can be placed in a document. So now you know what I mean by multimedia.

And now we come to what makes the World Wide Web unique—the hypertext part. Hypertext is a connection, sometimes called a **hot link,** that lets you jump from one document to another. Suppose you're reading a document that talks about the U.S. Department of Commerce and what it does. This document references, let's say, the Office of the President with a hypertext connection, or hot link. You click on the words *Office of the President* and see a new document that talks about the president.

So, to return to the original definition, the World Wide Web is simply a set of multimedia documents that are connected using hypertext links. And by clicking on the hot links, you can jump from one document to the next.

Before I finish this discussion, I should say two more quick things. First of all, to view a World Wide Web document, you need to have a Web browser. Microsoft Plus! for Windows 95 comes with a Web browser named **Internet Explorer**. But there are other popular Web browsers, including **Mosaic** and Netscape. Second, if you're new to the World Wide Web and don't know where to start, begin with the Web site *http:// www.yahoo.com*. It provides a directory of thousands of different World Wide Web servers.

If you want to get technical about hot links, read this

The documents you read, or view, with a Web browser are written using something called **HTML**. In fact, the Web browser client uses HTML instructions to display a document on your screen. These HTML instructions also include **uniform resource locators**. And when you click a hot link, the Web Browser client uses the uniform resource locator and the hypertext transfer protocol, or **HTTP,** to find and display the other document.

WWW ⁙ World Wide Web

ZIP   ZIP actually refers to a data-compression technique.
When people say a **file** is ZIPed, they usually mean it's
been compressed using the **PKZIP** utility. To use a ZIPed
file, you have to unZIP it. If a file has been ZIPed with
PKZIP, for example, you have to unZIP it with
PKUNZIP.

Zmodem When you download or upload a file using a communications application like **HyperTerminal,** you need to
choose a communications **protocol.** Zmodem, it turns
out, is one of the communications protocols you can
choose. If this were some dusty undergraduate telecom-
munications textbook, I'd probably launch into a detailed
technical discussion of the Zmodem protocol at this
point. But I'll save you the time. The one and only thing
you need to know about Zmodem is that it's a much
faster protocol than your other choices. So you'll want to
use it whenever you can.

⁙ **Downloading Files; Uploading Files**

TROUBLE-
SHOOTING

* *

Got a problem? Starting on the next page are solutions to the problems that plague new users of the Internet. You'll be on your way—and safely out of danger—in no time.

E-MAIL

You Don't Know Someone's E-Mail Address

You want to send so-and-so an **e-mail** message, but you don't have their address? Don't feel embarrassed. I think this is probably the most common Internet problem of all. Really. Fortunately, this problem is easy to solve.

Call them and ask

Sounds silly, doesn't it? But this really is the best solution. So go on and do it. You need to get both their **username** and the **domain name**. Once you know these bits of data, you just send your message to:

```
username@domainname
```

For example, if you wanted to send an e-mail message to me at my **America Online** address, you would send the message to:

```
StphnLNlsn@aol.com.
```

StphnLNlsn is my America Online username. And *aol.com* is the America Online domain name. If you're wondering where in the world I got my username, it's just my first name, middle initial, and last name, without any vowels.

E-mail the user's postmaster

If for some reason you can't call the person or contact them some other way—maybe a quick letter—you can also try e-mailing a request to the postmaster at the e-mail post office that serves the **host** on which your friend is a user. I'm not really sure this will work, by the way. Sometimes it will, sometimes it won't. What you're really doing is asking for a special favor from the person who administers the e-mail messaging system for the domain. But to do this, you can usually e-mail your message to:

```
postmaster@domainname
```

Of course, this means you need to know the domain name. So you may need to call the organization for that. But let's say you want to e-mail a message to an old school chum. You know he works for Parnell Aerospace in Taiwan, but you don't know his username. You need to call Parnell Aerospace and get the domain name of the Taiwan office—let's pretend it's *parnell.com.tw*. Then you e-mail your request to the following address:

```
postmaster@parnell.com.tw
```

FTP

You Can't Read a File You Downloaded

If you successfully **download a file** but discover you can't use it, your problem is almost certainly a "mode mixup." What's a mode mixup? When you move files with **FTP,** you move the files either in ASCII mode or in binary mode. Text files need to be moved in ASCII mode. Just about everything else needs to be moved in binary mode. If you use ASCII mode when you should have used binary mode, or vice versa, the file you get won't work right.

continues

You Can't Read a File You Downloaded *(continued)*

Try again with a different transfer mode

If you FTPed a file using the wrong mode, you can't do anything with the downloaded file. It's garbage. You may as well delete the downloaded file. Then try again using a different transfer mode. If you're not sure which transfer mode to use to download a file, take a peek at the table shown below. It describes my guess as to the best transfer mode to use for different kinds of files.

File	Type
ARC files	Binary
Database files	Binary
E-mail messages	ASCII
GIF files	Binary
Hypertext documents	ASCII
JPEG files	Binary
MPEG files	Binary
PKZIP files	Binary
PostScript files	ASCII
Program files	Binary
Source code files	ASCII
Spreadsheet files	Binary
Text files	ASCII
Uuencoded files	ASCII
Word processor files	Binary

To set the transfer mode when you're moving a file using FTP, use either the *ascii* command or the *binary* command. Type *ascii* to set the transfer mode to ASCII, of course. And type *binary* to set the transfer mode to binary.

WORLD WIDE WEB

You Can't Connect to a Web Server

If you can't connect to a Web server, either you've got the **uniform resource locator** (URL) wrong or the Web server isn't allowing you to connect—perhaps because it's over-worked and cranky. Unfortunately, both problems produce the same symptoms.

Check the uniform resource locator

Carefully check the uniform resource locator. The first part of the uniform resource locator should be *http://*. So make sure you've entered this part right. Note that the slashes are really slashes and not backslashes. The server name will probably look something like this: *www.microsoft.com*. In other words, it usually starts with the acronym *www* and then is followed by the Web server owner's **domain name**. So, to connect to Microsoft Corporation's Web server, you enter *http:// www.microsoft.com*. (Of course, if you're connecting to some other company's Web server, you don't enter *microsoft*.)

Be patient

Even if you've got the uniform resource locator entered correctly, you still may not be able to connect. If you get a message when you try to connect to a Web server that says something like "host not responding" or "host connection failed," it may just be that the Web server isn't available or is too busy to respond.

In this situation, your only real recourse is to try later. If the Web server is just really busy, by the way, you might be able to connect a few minutes later.

TELNET

You Can't Connect to a Host

If you can't connect to a **host** using the **Telnet** service, your problem probably boils down to one of two things: Either you've got the **uniform resource locator** (URL) wrong or the Telnet host isn't allowing you to connect. One of these situations you can do something about. The other you can't.

Check the uniform resource locator

If you get a message when you try to connect to a Telnet host that says something like "host unknown," you've got the wrong uniform resource locator. Plain and simple. So what you need to do is figure out the right uniform resource locator. Check your source document. Make sure you've entered it exactly as shown. If you did enter it correctly, either your source document is wrong or, just as likely, your source document is out of date.

Be patient

If you get a message when you try to connect to a Telnet host that says something like "host not responding" or "host connection failed," it may just be that the Telnet host isn't available right now. If you're trying to connect at some really crazy hour (like 3 a.m.) or when the Telnet host is really busy (like during prime business hours), the Telnet host is quite likely not available.

In this situation, your only real recourse is to try later. If you know what the Telnet host's usual hours of operation are and you know that the Telnet host is available, you might want to try again in, say, 10 minutes. If you're trying to connect to a Telnet host that you don't know much about or you're trying to connect at some crazy hour, it might be best to wait until normal working hours.

You Connect but Can't Log In or Issue Commands

This happened to me just the other day, in fact. I was showing the Internet to a friend. He wanted to Telnet to a library in Minnesota. Proudly I typed in the **uniform resource locator**. A few seconds later, the host we were trying to connect to responded. It asked for our **username** and a **password**. It was weird. I typed these in, successfully logged in, but then couldn't issue any commands. The Telnet host told me to type, for example, *HELP* to get a list of commands. So I typed *help*, but nothing happened. It told me I could type *MENU* to get a menu of commands. So I typed *menu*. Again, nothing.

Pay attention to whether your commands and entries should be uppercase or lowercase

You've probably already figured out what I was doing wrong. The case was important. The Telnet host wanted the word *HELP* and *MENU* in all capital letters. A command name in all lowercase letters like *help* or *menu* just wouldn't do the trick.

Actually, as a general comment, I'll also note that anytime you log in to a **server** running **UNIX**, the case is relevant. If the server wants all lowercase letters—and that's what it usually wants—you better type them. And, sometimes, when things are really crazy, the server wants uppercase letters. You had better type them, too.

You Can Issue Commands but You Don't See Them or You See Each Letter Twice

In the previous section, I started to tell you about the embarrassing little episode of Telnetting to a library in Minnesota. I have to tell you what happened next. As soon as I figured out the uppercase vs. lowercase business, I could type commands and get the Telnet host to do what I wanted it to. But when I typed the command, I wouldn't see it on the command prompt. I would type *HELP*, for example, but I wouldn't see anything. After I pressed Enter, however, I would see a screenful of help information. My friend, I feared, was rapidly losing confidence both in the Telnet service and in my abilities as a guide to **cyberspace**.

Adjust the local echo setting

What was wrong? The local echo setting. In my case, the Telnet client, Windows 95's Telnet program, needed to have the local echo setting turned on. To do this, you just choose the Terminal Preferences command. Then you mark the Local Echo check box.

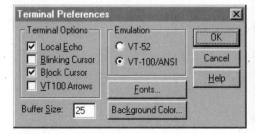

By the way, if you have local echo turned on when it should be turned off, you get double letters for just about everything. Rather than seeing a message like this:

```
Type HELP
```

You see a message like this:

```
TTyyppee HHEELLPP
```

If you get double letters, you should try turning off the local echo setting.

u Can't Discon-
ct from a Host

Once you've Telnetted to a host, you're connected. And you need to disconnect from it to get back to the host you started at. Disconnecting isn't difficult. But you do need to know the secret command or escape sequence to disconnect from the host.

Backtrack through the session log

When you initially connected to the host, the host almost certainly told you how to disconnect. If you're using something like **HyperTerminal,** which keeps a scrolling session log, you may be able to scroll backward and read the stuff you should have read when you first connected. HyperTerminal, by default, only keeps like the last 500 lines in the HyperTerminal application window. But you may as well try scrolling backward. Click above the HyperTerminal window's scroll bar marker to scroll backward.

Try all the old standbys

To quit whatever you're doing on the host computer, you can probably type an **escape character**. You might try Ctrl+]. You might also try Ctrl+C.

NEWSGROUPS

You Can't Access a Newsgroup You Want

The usual reason you can't access a **newsgroup** you want is that the system administrator has decided you shouldn't be able to access it. You may not be able to access it because the newsgroup's content isn't related to the organization's overall purpose. Or maybe the newsgroup's content is objectionable on political, philosophical, or religious grounds. So are you completely out of luck? No, probably not. There are a couple of things you can do when you're locked out.

Try another news server

A well-meaning system administrator can lock you out of a newsgroup in a couple of different ways. One way is to remove the newsgroup's **articles** from the news **server**. For example, if no articles are stored in the newsgroup *alt.really.inflammatory.commentaries*, you can't read them. (I just made up this newsgroup, by the way. It doesn't really exist. Or at least I don't think so.)

In this case, if you have a newsgroup reader that lets you specify the news server it reads and you know of another news server, you may be able to try the other news server. I don't know which newsgroup reader you're using. So I can't provide step-by-step instructions for specifying a different news server. But making this change shouldn't be too difficult.

Try another newsgroup reader

I mentioned earlier that there are two basic ways for system administrators to lock you out of newsgroups. One is to just not carry the newsgroup on the news server. The other way is to tell a newsgroup reader not to read a particular newsgroup. In the case of a **shell account** where the **access provider** supplies a newsgroup reader like **TIN**, this is how you get locked out. For the access provider, in this case, it's usually easiest to tell the newsgroup reader to just ignore certain newsgroups.

In this case, you may still be able to read articles in this newsgroup by using another newsgroup reader—such as a newsgroup reader **client** running on your PC. So if you can't access a newsgroup and you're using a newsgroup reader client on the access provider's computer, you might want to try this.

You Can't Decode a Picture or Binary File

I find that I'm usually pretty successful decoding binary files. But sometimes my usual method doesn't work right. I have a shell account as one of the ways I connect, for example. And when I use TIN's decoding command, I sometimes can't get it to work (it does work most of the time). I think the problem is that some encoding/decoding utilities are a little quirky. (Either that, I guess, or some of the people encoding binary files are a little quirky.) Whatever or whoever is the culprit, there are minor differences in the ways that binary files get encoded. When a utility isn't smart enough to deal with these little subtleties, the decoding often doesn't work.

continues

You Can't Decode a Picture or Binary File *(continued)*

Try another encoding/decoding utility

When I can't use one decoding utility, I usually find that I can use another one. For example, when TIN's utility doesn't work, one of the **shareware** or freeware utilities almost always does. You can usually find these utilities in newsgroups such as *alt.binaries.pictures.utilities.*

If you can find one of these utilities, **download** it, and successfully decode it (using your regular decoding utility). You'll usually be able to decode a file this way. (What's probably happening if this does work, by the way, is that you're getting a newer or smarter encoding/decoding utility.)

An obvious suggestion?

I probably should have mentioned this first, but you may as well also try decoding another, different binary file too. Be sure to try a binary file that's been posted by someone other than the poster of the binary file you're having trouble with. Very possibly, whoever or whatever encoded the file you're having trouble with goofed it up in some way.

Your Picture Looks Gritty

Let's say you've downloaded a picture. You decoded the thing. You've successfully opened it using a **viewer.** But your picture looks really gritty. You can sort of make out what you're supposed to see, but the picture is nowhere close to being photograph quality. This, you're wondering to yourself, is what everybody is getting so excited about?

Increase the number of colors and the resolution

To view photographic images on your monitor, you need to use a Super VGA monitor. Super VGA monitors provide greater resolution and display more colors. And you need to tell Windows 95 to use high resolution and a bunch of color. You probably have a Super VGA monitor if you purchased your monitor anytime in the last few years. But there's a good chance that you're not using its high resolution and color capabilities. To make sure you are, follow these steps:

1 Double-click on the Windows 95 desktop. Windows 95 displays a menu of commands related to the **desktop.**

2 Choose the Properties command. Windows 95 displays the Display Properties dialog box.

3 Click the Settings tab.

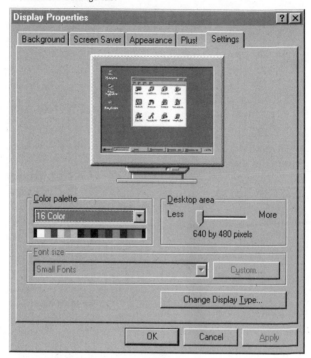

4 If the Color Palette drop-down list box shows 16 Color, select a higher color setting, such as 256 color, High Color (16-bit), or True Color (24-bit). The higher the color setting you choose, the more colors you'll see and the better the image quality will be.

5 Use the Desktop Area slide control to increase the resolution. You drag the slide area tool right to do this.

6 Click OK. Windows 95 may ask if it can reboot your computer so the display setting changes can take effect. You may as well do this.

continues

Your Picture Looks Gritty *(continued)*

Try another picture

Some of the pictures that get posted aren't high-quality photographic images. So if you've verified that you're using a lot of color and a high resolution, download some other images. Quite likely the grittiness you're seeing is in the image itself and is not the result of a problem with your computer or viewer.

HYPERTERMINAL

Your Files Take a Long Time to Download or Upload

It's a bummer, isn't it? You want—no, you need—a particular file. And you need it now. But it's taking forever and a day to **download.** Is there anything you can do to speed things up? You bet there is.

Use a fast protocol

One of the best things about the new **HyperTerminal** application that comes with Windows 95 is that it provides the fast **Zmodem** protocol (fast, that is, compared to the old **Terminal** application that came with the earlier versions of Windows). Zmodem is faster for a couple of reasons. One is that it's just faster at transmitting data. Plain and simple. Another reason it's faster is that you can tell it to download a bunch of different files at once. You don't have to take the time to individually download a single file at a time.

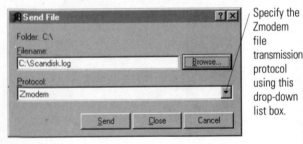

Specify the Zmodem file transmission protocol using this drop-down list box.

Compress the files you want to move

You won't get much compression on graphic image files like **GIF** and **JPEG** files. But on most other files you can considerably shrink the file if you use a data-compression utility like **PKZIP.** Smaller files upload and download more quickly. Duh.

Multitask so you can do something else

When you sit in front of a monitor watching the progress of a file transmission, it can seem pretty darn slow. But remember that you don't have to just sit and wait. With Windows 95, you can easily open more than one application. Let's say, for example, that you have some work you want to do in Microsoft Word. You can start **downloading files** (using the Zmodem protocol, of course!), then open up a Word document and work with it. As you do your Word work, HyperTerminal is busy downloading your files. Perhaps a few pages later, all your stuff is downloaded. And maybe most of that report is written, too.

QUICK REFERENCE

●●●

Any time you explore some exotic location, you're bound to see flora and fauna you can't identify. To be sure you can identify the commands and toolbar buttons you see in the Internet clients that come with Windows 95 and Plus!, the Quick Reference describes these items in systematic detail.

FTP CLIENT COMMANDS

Command	Description
!	Escapes to the shell.
?	Prints help information about the FTP client application.
append	Appends one file to another (e.g., *append file1 file2* tacks file1 onto the end of file2).
ascii	Sets the file transfer type to ASCII so you can send or receive an ASCII, or text, file.
bell	Tells the FTP client to sound a bell or buzzer whenever it completes a command. (To turn off the bell, issue the bell command again.)
binary	Sets the file transfer type to binary so you can send or receive a binary file.
bye	Terminates an FTP session and closes the FTP client application.
cd	Changes the working directory on the host you FTPed to. (This pretty much works like the MS-DOS command of same name.)
close	Terminates an FTP session without closing the FTP client application.
debug	Turns on or off the FTP's debugging mode.
delete	Deletes a *file* on the host you FTPed to.
dir	Lists the contents of the working directory on the host you FTPed to. (Works like the MS-DOS command of same name.)
disconnect	Terminates an FTP session without closing the FTP client application.
get	Retrieves a specified file from the working directory of the host you've FTPed to (e.g., *get file1* retrieves the file named *file1* from the remote host and then stores it in the working directory of your PC).

Command	Description
glob	Turns metacharacter expansion of local file names on or off.
hash	Turns the printing of a pound sign (#) for each buffer transferred on or off.
help	Displays a list of commands. (If you type *help* followed by the command name, help displays a short command description.)
lcd	Changes the local host's working directory—in other words, the active directory on your PC.
literal	Sends arbitrary FTP commands.
ls	lists the contents of the remote host's working directory. Similar to the DIR command.
mdelete	Deletes a group of (multiple) files on the remote host.
mdir	Lists the contents of multiple directories on the remote host.
mget	Retrieves multiple files from the remote host.
mkdir	Makes a directory on the remote host. (Works like the MS-DOS command of the same name.)
mls	lists the contents of multiple directories on the remote host.
mput	Sends multiple files.
open	Connects to a remote FTP site.
prompt	Tells FTP to interactively prompt you when you're issuing multiple commands.
put	Sends a file.
pwd	Displays the name of the working directory on the remote host.
quit	Terminates the FTP session and closes the FTP client application.
quote	Sends arbitrary FTP commands.

continues

FTP Client Commands *(continued)*

Command	Description
recv	Receives a file.
remotehelp	Gets help from the remote host.
rename	Renames a file. (Works like the MS-DOS command of the same name.)
rmdir	Removes directory on the remote host.
send	Sends a file.
status	Shows the current status of the FTP session.
trace	Turns the tracking of packets on or off.
type	Sets the file transfer type.
user	Sends new information about you to the remote host.
verbose	Turns the verbose mode on or off.

INTERNET EXPLORER COMMANDS

File Menu

Open...	Opens a file you created by previously saving a Web page.
Open Start Page...	Opens your starting, or home, Web page.
Save As...	Saves current Web page to your hard disk.
Create Shortcut	Creates a shortcut icon for the current page and adds it to the desktop.
Page Setup...	Specifies how Web pages should be printed.
Print	Prints the current Web page.
Exit	Closes, or stops, the Internet Explorer applicaton.

About the numbered File menu commands

The File menu also lists as numbered commands the Web pages you've viewed during the current Web session. To move to one of these pages, choose its numbered menu command.

Edit Menu

Cut	Removes the current selection and places it on the Clipboard so you can paste the selection somewhere else.
Copy	Makes a copy of the current selection and places the copy on the Clipboard so you can paste the selection somewhere else.
Paste	Moves the selection currently stored on the Clipboard to the insertion point.
Select All	Selects all the text in the window.
Find...	Searches for specified text on the current Web page.

View Menu

Back	Goes back to the previous Web page.
Forward	Goes forward to the next Web page.
Toolbar	Adds or removes a toolbar from the window. (Internet Explorer marks the command with a check mark when the toolbar is present.)
Address Bar	Adds or removes the URL (uniform resource locator) address bar from the window. (Internet Explorer marks the command with a check mark when the address bar is present.)
Status Bar	Adds or removes a status bar from the window. (Internet Explorer also marks the command with a check mark when the status bar is present.)

continues

View Menu *(continued)*

Fonts	Displays the Font submenu:	
	Largest	Uses 12-point text in the window.
	Large	Uses 11-point text in the window.
	Medium	Uses 10-point text in the window.
	Small	Uses 9-point text in the window.
	Smallest	Uses 8-point text in the window.
Stop	Tells Internet Explorer to stop whatever it's doing—such as retrieving a web page.	
Refresh	Tells Internet Explorer to read the Web page again (from the Web server) and then redraw the window.	
Options...	Displays the Options dialog box so you can specify how the Internet Explorer works.	

Favorites Menu

Add To Favorites...	Adds the current Web page location to a list of favorite places.
Open Favorites	Displays the Favorites folder, which lists your favorite Web pages.

About the other Favorites menu commands

The Favorites menu also lists the favorite places you've already added by using the Add To Favorites command. To move to one of these pages, choose its menu command.

Help Menu

Help Topics	Displays the Help Topics dialog box.
About...	Displays the About Internet Explorer dialog box and gives the available memory and system resources.

INTERNET EXPLORER TOOLBAR GUIDE

	Opens a file you created by previously saving a Web page.
	Opens your Web home base, or home page.
	Goes back to the previous Web page.
	Goes forward to the next Web page.
	Tells Internet Explorer to stop whatever it's doing—such as retrieving a Web page from some distant Web server.
	Tells Internet Explorer to read the Web page again (from the Web server) and then redraw the window.
	Displays the Favorites folder, which lists all your favorite Web pages.
	Adds the current Web page location to a list of favorite places.
	Tells Internet Explorer to display the text in the window in a larger font size.
	Tells Internet Explorer to display the text in the window in a smaller font size.
	Removes the current selection and places it on the Clipboard so you can paste the selection somewhere else.
	Makes a copy of the current selection and places the copy on the Clipboard so you can paste the selection somewhere else.
	Moves the selection currently stored on the Clipboard to the insertion point.

HYPERTERMINAL COMMAND GUIDE

File Menu

New Connection Displays dialog boxes for describing a new HyperTerminal connection.

Open... Opens a HyperTerminal connection you've previously described and saved.

Save Saves a HyperTerminal connection or any changes you've made to a HyperTerminal connection.

Save As... Saves a HyperTerminal connection for the first time or renames an existing HyperTerminal connection.

Page Setup... Describes how HyperTerminal should print session information.

Print... Tells HyperTerminal to print the session information—the stuff that appears in the HyperTerminal application window.

Properties... Displays a dialog box you can use to view and change the properties of a HyperTerminal session.

Exit Closes, or stops, the HyperTerminal application.

Edit Menu

Copy Copies the selected text in the HyperTerminal application window to the Windows 95 Clipboard.

Paste To Host Pastes the contents of the Windows 95 Clipboard into the HyperTerminal application window, effectively sending the Clipboard's contents to the access provider's computer.

Select All Selects the entire contents of the HyperTerminal application window.

View Menu

Toolbar Tells HyperTerminal to display or not display its toolbar.

Status Bar Tells HyperTerminal to display or not display its status bar.

Font... Displays a dialog box for choosing which font HyperTerminal uses inside its application window.

Call Menu

Connect Tells HyperTerminal to connect to another computer, such as your access provider's.

Disconnect Tells HyperTerminal to disconnect from the computer it's already connected to.

Transfer Menu

Send File... Tells HyperTerminal to send a file on your PC to the other computer.

Receive File... Tells HyperTerminal to grab and save a file sent by the other computer you're connected to.

Capture Text... Grabs all the incoming text you see flying across the HyperTerminal application window and saves the text in a file.

Send Text File... Tells HyperTerminal to send a text file to the other computer you're connected to.

Capture To Printer Grabs all the incoming text you see flying across the HyperTerminal application window and prints it.

Help Menu

Help Topics Lists the major help topic categories.

About HyperTerminal... Displays the copyright notice, the software version number, and system information from your computer.

HyperTerminal Toolbar Guide

Displays dialog boxes for describing a new HyperTerminal connection.

Opens a HyperTerminal connection you've previously described and saved.

Tells HyperTerminal to connect to another computer, such as your access provider's.

Tells HyperTerminal to disconnect from the computer it's already connected to.

Tells HyperTerminal to send a file on your PC to the other computer.

Tells HyperTerminal to grab and save a file sent by the other computer you're connected to.

Displays a dialog box for viewing and changing the properties of a HyperTerminal session.

Microsoft Exchange Command Guide

File

Open	Displays contents of selected folder or e-mail message.
Save As...	Saves selected e-mail message in a different folder.
Move...	Moves selected e-mail message to another folder.
Copy...	Copies selected e-mail message to another folder.
Print...	Prints selected e-mail message.
New Folder...	Creates a new folder.
Delete	Deletes selected folder or e-mail message.
Rename	Renames selected folder.

Properties	Displays or changes properties of selected folder or e-mail message.
Import...	Imports a Microsoft Mail file or Personal Address Book so you can use it from inside of Exchange.
Exit	Closes the Microsoft Exchange application and any other messaging applications using Microsoft Exchange.
Exit and Logoff	Closes the Microsoft Exchange application and any other messaging applications using Microsoft Exchange.

Edit

Select All	Selects all the folders or e-mail messages shown in the message pane.
Mark As Read	Marks the selected message as one you've read.
Mark As Unread	Unmarks a message you've previously marked as read.

View

Folder	Turns off and on the display of the folders pane (Command is checked if folders pane is displayed).
Toolbar	Turns off and on the display of the toolbar (Command is checked if toolbar is displayed).
Status Bar	Turns off and on the display of the status bar (Command is checked if status bar is displayed).
New Window	Opens another, new Microsoft Exchange window.
Columns...	Displays a dialog box you use to specify what information you want displayed in the message pane.
Sort...	Displays a dialog box you use to specify how messages should be arranged.

Tools

Deliver Now	Sends all the e-mail messages in your Outbox folder.
Address Book	Displays the address book, a list of e-mail addresses.
Find...	Looks for an e-mail message matching a specified description.
Remote Mail...	Opens the Remote Mail window so you can transmit and receive.
Customize Toolbar...	Lets you add and remove toolbar buttons.
Ser**v**ices...	Lets you change the way your Internet mail service and connection works.
Options...	Changes Exchange's appearance and operation.

Compose

New Message	Opens the New Message window so you can whip up a quick e-mail message.
WordMail Options...	Changes the way the WordMail e-mail editor works. (This command only appears if WordMail is your editor.)
Reply To Sender	Creates a new message that replies to the sender of the currently displayed message.
Reply To **A**ll	Creates a new message that replies to all the recipients of the currently displayed message.
Forward	Sends a copy of the currently displayed message to someone new.

Help

Microsoft Exchange Help Topics	Starts Help and opens the file of Microsoft Exchange help information.
Internet Mail Help Topics	Starts Help and opens the file of Internet Mail client help information.
About Microsoft Exchange	Displays the copyright notice and the software version number.

TELNET COMMAND GUIDE

Connect Menu

Remote System...	Displays a dialog box for naming the Telnet host you want to connect to.
Disconnect	Disconnects your PC from the Telnet host you're connected to.
Exit	Closes, or stops, the Telnet application.

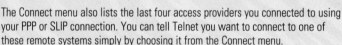

About the numbered Connect menu commands

The Connect menu also lists the last four access providers you connected to using your PPP or SLIP connection. You can tell Telnet you want to connect to one of these remote systems simply by choosing it from the Connect menu.

Edit Menu

Copy	Copies the selected text in the Telnet application window to the Windows 95 Clipboard.
Paste	Pastes the contents of the Windows 95 Clipboard into the Telnet application window.
Select All	Selects the entire contents of the Telnet application window.

Terminal Menu

Preferences...   Displays a dialog box you can use to specify how the Telnet application window should look and how the Telnet application itself should work.

Start Logging...   Saves all the stuff that appears in the Telnet application window to a log named telnet.log. You can open the log file using a word processor, Notepad, or WordPad.

Stop Logging   Tells Telnet to stop keeping a session log.

Help Menu

Contents   Lists the major help topic categories.

Search for Help On...   Provides help on a topic you specify.

How to Use Help   Provides help on the Help application.

About Telnet   Displays the copyright notice, the software version number, and system information from your computer.

G

H

The manuscript for this book was prepared and submitted to Microsoft Press in electronic form. Text files were prepared using Microsoft Word 6.0 for Windows. Pages were composed by Stephen L. Nelson, Inc., using PageMaker 5.0 for Windows, with text in Minion and display type in Copperplate. Composed pages were delivered to the printer as electronic prepress files.

COVER DESIGNER
Rebecca Geisler-Johnson

COVER ILLUSTRATOR
Eldon Doty

INTERIOR TEXT DESIGNER
The Understanding Business

ENVIRONMENT ILLUSTRATIONS
Stefan Knorr

PAGE LAYOUT AND TYPOGRAPHY
Stefan Knorr

COPY EDITOR
Peter Weverka

TECHNICAL EDITOR
Beth Shannon

INDEXER
Julie Kawabata

Printed on recycled paper stock.